Mums *who* Clean

The inspiration for Mums Who came in early 2017 with a Facebook message about home organisation. After realising how much they had in common, Karlie and Rachael became great friends and together set up the Mums Who brand, starting with the Mums Who Organise Facebook group. The Mums Who Clean Facebook group was formed after many requests and quickly became their most popular group. Karlie and Rachael now have eleven Mums Who groups on Facebook, all providing safe, friendly and supportive communities where Australian women can share their ideas, strategies and hacks.

Both small business owners based in Victoria, Karlie has three daughters and Rachael is a mother of two boys.

mumswho.com.au
facebook.com/groups/mumswhoclean
@MumsWhoAU
@mumswhoau

All the best advice,
hacks and products for
quick and easy cleaning

Mums *who* Clean

Rachael Hallett & Karlie Suttie

EBURY
PRESS

EBURY PRESS

UK | USA | Canada | Ireland | Australia
India | New Zealand | South Africa | China

Ebury Press is part of the Penguin Random House group of companies
whose addresses can be found at global.penguinrandomhouse.com

Penguin
Random House
Australia

First published by Ebury Press in 2021

While the utmost care has been taken in researching and compiling this book,
the information it contains is a guide only. Readers should check manufacturers'
care instructions for individual items they wish to clean, spot-test, and ensure the power
is turned off before cleaning items with electrical components.

Readers should also store all cleaning products and essential oils out of reach of children and pets.
Essential oils, while natural, can be toxic to both humans and animals if ingested or inhaled.

Cover and internal design by Adam Laszczuk © Penguin Random House Australia Pty Ltd
Typeset in 11.5/18 pt Neutraface Text by Post Pre-press

Printed and bound in China by 1010 Printing

 A catalogue record for this
book is available from the
NATIONAL LIBRARY OF AUSTRALIA   National Library of Australia

ISBN 978 1 76104 213 3

penguin.com.au

Contents

· · · · · · · · · · · · · · · ·

about
this
book

how to get the most out
of Mums Who Clean

about **Rachael**

. . . .

MY NAME IS RACHAEL and I am the mother of two boys, the wife of Tim, a business owner, a Mums Who co-creator and now an author!

I love cooking, budgeting, doing super fun stuff with my kids and relaxing at the movies with Tim. (Sorry but I don't *love* cleaning!)

about **Karlie**

. . . .

MY NAME IS KARLIE and I live in Victoria with my husband and three daughters. I am a small-business owner, Mums Who co-creator and, with this book, an author.

I love spending time with my friends, my family and especially my girls. I thrive on being busy and completing little projects, which is probably why I don't have as much time to relax as I would like. If cleaning took any longer I would never do it, which is why I always look for the easiest way possible!

about **Mums Who**

· · · · · · · · · · · · · · ·

THE INSPIRATION FOR MUMS WHO came in early 2017 with a Facebook message we exchanged (we were strangers at the time) – a simple message about our love of home organisation. After realising how much we had in common, we began an amazing friendship, and together we set up the Mums Who brand.

Soon after, we created the Mums Who Organise Facebook group. This new group enabled women to share their ideas, strategies and hacks in a safe, friendly and supportive community.

We never imagined that it would lead us so far in such a short time. Members joined, and then more, and then even more!

Requests for new groups on different topics flooded in, and Mums Who Clean was formed. We were stunned when it quickly became our most popular group.

We now have eleven Mums Who groups on Facebook, as well as an official Mums Who Facebook page and Instagram account.

The most exciting part of the Mums Who journey happened in late 2019, when the idea of a Mums Who Clean book was raised. For two people who had never even thought about writing a book, this was an amazing opportunity. We wanted to share what we had learned with others.

Although not many of us actually like cleaning, we hope that this book gives you tips and ideas on how to make cleaning an easier part of your daily life.

how to **Use This Book**

· · · · · · · · · · · · · · · · ·

THIS BOOK IS DESIGNED to help you and your family spring-clean your home.

You might like to clean room by room, or complete one type of task at a time. This guide can help with both strategies of cleaning.

We have split the main cleaning into two parts. You can read through the General Cleaning chapter and use those techniques as you clean room by room. Or, if you prefer, you can clean each of the items or features in your home individually before you start a room-by-room clean.

Completing the General Cleaning tasks first is likely to be more efficient. However, you may struggle with a lack of motivation – in that case, going room by room might be best for you.

If you are a bit overwhelmed, skip forward to the My Home is Out of Control chapter to get started.

After the General Cleaning chapter and the room-by-room chapters, you will find advice on real-estate cleaning, how to create a cleaning schedule, and cleaning recipes. You'll also find space to jot down tips and tricks from the book or from the Mums Who community.

Of course, though our fantastic online community includes many women, cleaning shouldn't automatically fall to mums or indeed any one person within a household. We are Mums Who, not Mums Have To! Sharing the responsibilities will definitely make it quicker and easier, and this is where our cleaning schedule comes in especially handy. Making it a family effort will lighten the load!

This cleaning companion will help you to get your house in order and keep it that way, no matter how you decide to use this book. We hope you enjoy the advice and tips we offer.

Good luck and best wishes,

Rachael and *Karlie*

top
cleaning products and tools

members' and personal favourites
to help you get your cleaning done
with less effort

from **Mums Who Clean**

· · · · · · · · · · · · · · · · ·

THESE ARE THE PRODUCTS THAT Mums Who Clean members can't get enough of! Some of these products just work so well that our members love using them as they were designed to be used. Others are existing products that our members have found fantastic new uses for.

Make sure you read the manufacturer's instructions on the product before trying any hints or tips. Some products may not be suitable for use on every appliance, model or surface.

· ·

Baby Wipes

- Venetian blinds
- Window tracks
- Skirting boards
- Screen doors
- Walls

Use a baby wipe in the same way as you would use a cloth. Wipe over the areas that are affected and discard the wipes appropriately (do not flush).

Rachael's *tip*
Biodegradable or reusable wipes are a more eco-friendly solution.

· ·

Bar Keepers Friend Cleanser & Polish Powder

- Barbecue exterior
- Shower screens
- Kitchen sink
- Stainless steel appliances

Sprinkle the powder onto the surface to be cleaned. Use a wet cloth to wipe vigorously, removing any blemishes and shining the surface.

Alternatively, you can sprinkle the powder directly onto the wet cloth.

This product may scratch so ensure you read the packaging and use only on appropriate surfaces.

- -

Biozet Attack Laundry Liquid

- **Tiled floors**

Add a very small amount to your mop bucket, and mop as normal. Avoid adding too much or the floor may become slippery.

- **Urine or vomit smell on fabrics, upholstery and carpets**

Fill a spray bottle with water and add a small squirt of Biozet to the water. Spray onto your fabric, upholstery or carpet. Use a soft brush or cloth to work the product in and wipe away with a damp cloth.

- -

Bissell SpotClean

- **Small stains on carpets/rugs**
- **Stains on lounges**

This portable upholstery-cleaning machine is great at removing stains. Refer to the user manual for your machine.

- -

Bosisto's Multipurpose Cleaner

- **Shower screens**
- **Benchtops**
- **Furniture**

Use spray as per package instructions.

Di-San Pre Wash Stain Remover

- Tile grout
- Shower screens
- Stains on clothing
- Stains on carpets
- Greasy areas

Spray the affected areas and use an appropriate scrubbing brush or cloth to work in the product. Wipe or mop away the excess.

Dishwasher Tablets

- **Oven door**

Wearing thick rubber gloves, dip a dishwasher tablet into water and use the tablet to scrub the grime off the interior of your oven door. Wipe with a clean cloth to remove any residue.

- **Oven racks**

Remove the racks from your oven and wrap each one loosely in aluminium foil. Put all the racks into a bath or tub of hot water. Drop in 1 dishwasher tablet per rack and let soak until the water is cold.

Use a small scourer or cloth to wipe over each rack, and the build-up will wipe away.

- **Pots/saucepans with burnt-on material**

Fill the pot with hot water and drop in 1–2 dishwasher tablets. Allow to soak overnight and clean as normal.

- **Stainless steel laundry tub/trough**

Place the plug in your tub/trough and line the walls and base with aluminium foil. Place 3 or 4 tablets into the tub and fill with hot water. Leave the water for a few hours. Discard the foil and give the tub a light scrub before draining the water. This will leave your tub looking almost new again.

- **Washing machine drum clean**

Place 4 tablets into the drum of your washing machine, close the door and run a long, hot machine cycle. To avoid a stale smell after cleaning, ensure you clean out the machine's filter. Refer to your washing machine's user manual for recommended cleaning advice, and check with your manufacturer before putting dishwasher tablets into the machine.

· ·

Dr. Beckmann Carpet Stain Remover

- **Stains on carpet**
- **Stains on fabric lounges**

Use as per package instructions.

· ·

Earth Choice Bath & Shower Rapid Clean

- **Bathrooms**

Use as per package instructions.

· ·

Scalex Heavy Duty Home Descaler

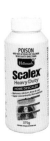

- **Heavy deposits in showers**

Dilute 1 tablespoon of powder into 100 ml of warm water and put in a spray bottle. Spray the affected areas and let sit for 10 minutes before using a scrubbing brush to remove the deposits.

- **Toilet bowl**

Pour ⅓ cup of Scalex into the toilet bowl and leave overnight if possible.

Koh Universal Cleaner

- Windows
- Stainless steel
- Glass furniture
- Oven

Use as per package instructions.

Lemons

- **Barbecue**

After cooking, sprinkle some table salt or cooking salt onto the warm hotplate. Then, using the cut side of half a lemon, rub the salt over the hotplate. Wipe up with an old cloth or paper towels.

- **Kettle**

Slice or quarter a fresh lemon and place 1 or 2 pieces into your kettle. Fill the kettle with water, bring to the boil and leave to cool.

Once cool, pour out the water and discard the lemon. If required, give the inside a quick wipe with a cloth, or with a bottle brush if you have one. Fill your kettle with fresh water and boil again. Discard the water.

Rachael's *tip*
Freeze any leftover lemon to use next time.

Long Life Grout Cleaner

- Grout

Use as per package instructions.

Magic Eraser

Ensure you spot-test as the eraser may remove or damage some surfaces.

- Walls
- Doors
- Skirting boards
- Cabinets

Wet the eraser and use it to remove any marks.

- **Oven door**

Wet the eraser and use it to scrub the surface of your oven door.

- **Shoes**

Wet the eraser and use it to remove any marks on the rubber soles.

- **Stovetop**

Wet the eraser and use it to scrub any marks on the surface of the stove, and on the burner sections on a gas stove. Take care to avoid any markings on the knobs.

- **Tiles**

Wet the eraser and use it to scrub the surface of your tiles. It can be used over the whole tiled area or for spot-cleaning.

One Shot Thick Concentrated Acidic Toilet Bowl Cleaner

- **Scale on toilet bowl**

Squirt a generous amount of product into and around your toilet bowl. Use your toilet brush to scrub the product and let rest for 30 minutes. Flush the toilet to remove any residue – use the brush again if required.

Orange Power Sticky Spot & Goo Dissolver

- **Stickers**
- **Kids' drawings on walls**
- **Sticky residue**
- **Glass bakeware**

Use as per package instructions.

Polident 3 Minute Daily Cleanser Tablets

Make up a Polident solution (see Cleaning Recipes).

- **Fabric**

Spray the solution onto the fabric and wash as normal, or wipe vigorously with a soft brush or cloth.

- **Grout**

Spray the solution onto tile grout and use a grout brush to scrub the areas. Mop up once complete to remove any residue and dirty water.

- **Shoes**

Spray or soak the shoes with the Polident solution before scrubbing with a nailbrush. Rinse thoroughly or wash in the washing machine before use.

- **Tiled floor**

Pour the solution all over the floor and move it around with a soft broom to cover the whole surface. You may need quite a bit of mixture depending on the size of the area. Leave the mixture for 10–20 minutes. If you have an all-in-one vacuum/mop (e.g. a Bissell CrossWave or similar), you can use this to lift grime and the Polident mixture off the floor. You can also use a spin mop or another type of mop that is easy to wring.

Shaving Foam

- **Smelly grout (around the toilet, from urine)**

Spread shaving foam over the affected floor tiles and around the base of the toilet, where it meets the floor. Leave the foam on the floor for 30 minutes and then mop with hot water to remove the residue. The shaving foam will remove any urine smells.

from **Rachael**

. . . .

- **COBWEB BROOM:** Any brand works. Mine is from Kmart.

- **BISSELL CROSSWAVE CORDLESS:** This all-in-one vacuum/mop, with cleaning formula, is amazing on hard floors and rugs. It mops and vacuums at the same time, and we love the way it saves us time and physical effort.

- **DUSTER:** I use a Kmart brand one with an extendable handle. I am pretty short, so the extendable handle is important for me.

- **DYSON V11 OUTSIZE PRO CORDLESS STICK VACUUM:** I love that this vacuum is wall mounted for charging so I can hang it in my broom closet. It also has great suction and leaves all surfaces really clean.

- **ESSENTIAL OILS:** Essential oils add amazing smells and aid in the cleaning process. A few I love to use are:

  - **Lemon –** I use a couple of drops of this in my Koh bottle when I feel like adding scent to my cleaning routine.
  - **Eucalyptus –** This is another great option for adding scent to the Koh cleaner. It's also fantastic for removing sticky messes from various surfaces.
  - **Lavender –** This is a really great one to add to your washing machine. If I've accidentally left clothes in the machine too long, I fill my fabric softener drawer with white vinegar, add a couple of drops of lavender oil and rewash. It really gets rid of the musty smell.

Note

Use essential oils with caution. Some may be toxic to pets and to people.

- **HAIRSPRAY:** Great for stubborn scuff marks.

- **NATURE DIRECT ENVIROMIST:** I use this for controlling odours in the air. It is the most effective air-freshening product I've ever used.

- **NATURE DIRECT TOUGH GUY CLOTH:** This is the best cloth for my matt kitchen cabinets.

- **PAINT SCRAPER OR LONG-HANDLED FLOOR SCRAPER:** I use one of these to remove sticky stuff off the floor while mopping. Better than scraping with my thumbnail!

- **RUBBERMAID REVEAL SPRAY MOP:** This is wonderful for cleaning right to the corners and small areas of a floor while using the Bissell CrossWave mop.

- **WHITE MAGIC SCRUBTASTIC FOAM POT SCRUBBER:** Excellent for hard hand-scrubbing of dishes and surfaces.

from **Karlie**

- **BISSELL SPOTCLEAN TURBO:** I love this little machine. I use it for cleaning my couch and occasional chairs, and for little spills on rugs, carpets and mattresses. It is especially amazing if you are toilet-training a child and a whoopsie makes it onto the floor – the Turbo makes cleaning it up so easy.

- **HAIR DRYER:** This is perfect for heating stickers or labels for easy removal. Also really helpful for cleaning a toaster. Yes, you read that right . . .

- **HIZERO CORDLESS BIONIC MOP:**
  This machine is amazing for cleaning up all kinds of messes on hard floors. It is especially useful for cleaning up after dinner, when the kids have made a mess on the floor. It sweeps up debris while also mopping up spills.

- **POWER OF 4 LAUNDRY POWDER:**
  I don't use this for all my clothes, but it is amazing for white clothing and bed linen. It brings discoloured whites back to life.

- **TRUEECO EVERYDAY CLEANER:**
  I particularly like this versatile cleaner for glass, shower screens and mirrors. It has other uses too.

- **WHITE MAGIC ECO BASICS DISH BRUSH:** This brush made from bamboo and recycled plastic is great for removing stuck-on food scraps.

- **WHITE MAGIC COMPACT SPRAY MOP:** I have two microfibre pads – one for floors, and one for walls and small spills. This mop is much lighter than other spray mops and the head is very easy to manoeuvre, which I love.

- **WHITE MAGIC ECO CLOTH MICROFIBRE CLOTHS:** I love this range of microfibre cloths. I have seven that I rotate through.

we Both Love . . .

- **BICARBONATE OF SODA (BICARB):** Bicarb is a super cheap and effective cleaning product – a little goes a long way. It cuts down on cleaning effort, which is a plus. It can be used as a light abrasive on sinks, cabinets and benchtops and is great at removing odours.

- **BISSELL PROHEAT 2X REVOLUTION PET:** This carpet- and upholstery-cleaning machine is great for keeping carpets, mattresses and couches clean. If you have spilled something, this machine sucks the liquid right out of the upholstery or carpet.

- **KOH UNIVERSAL CLEANER:** This cleaning product can be used for almost everything that needs to be sprayed. It's non-toxic and has no scent unless you add essential oils, which makes it a lovely product to use.

- **STRUCKET:** The strainer-meets-bucket is a fabulous Australian invention that takes the hassle out of soaking and handwashing laundry. But it also has so many other uses – washing toys, storing bath toys, and even cleaning fruit and veggies in the kitchen. Its versatility is one of the reasons we love it so much.

- **WHITE MAGIC DISH DRYING MAT:** Use this instead of (or under) a rack for drying dishes. It's really fabulous for catching run-off and protecting benchtops.

- **WHITE MAGIC ECO CLOTH TEA TOWELS:** These are *amazing*. They dry so effectively and leave zero annoying lint. An absolute must-have.

- **WHITE MAGIC WASHING UP PAD:** This is great for wiping benchtops and chopping boards, and for doing dishes by hand.

- **WHITE VINEGAR:** This is such a cheap and versatile product. It's definitely a cleaning must-have. It can be used for glass, stainless steel and drains, though avoid leaving it on stainless steel for long periods of time, as it can corrode the surface if not wiped up.

general cleaning

how to best clean the main

surfaces throughout your home

CLEANING YOUR HOME CAN BE A DAUNTING TASK. If you haven't done it in a while, or if you're short on time, you may feel overwhelmed and unsure where to begin. These general cleaning tips will help you clean the items and features that are found in most rooms.

Cornices

• • • • • • • • • • • • • • • •

OFTEN FORGOTTEN AS THEY ARE HIGH and beyond our daily line of sight, cornices need regular attention to avoid build-up of cobwebs, dust and dead insects. A cobweb broom is the perfect tool to make this job quick and easy.

Run the cobweb broom over your cornice to remove dust and cobwebs. Swipe across the top of doorjambs and windowsills, down wall corners and inside window frames. You may also like to use this time to go over any areas in your home where cobwebs are common. Then, using a clean, damp cloth, wipe any marks you have found. If you can't reach the cornices, use a sturdy stepladder.

Ceiling Fans

• • • • • • • • • • • • • • • •

ENSURE FANS ARE SWITCHED OFF. A cobweb broom is the easiest tool to remove cobwebs and dust from the top of ceiling fan blades but it will not clean them completely. Use a stepladder to access the top of the blades, spray some general-purpose spray on a damp cloth and wipe them down.

Air Ducts, Vents *and* Return Air

USE A DUSTER TO REMOVE AS MUCH DUST as you can from the duct cover. If there are any marks on the cover, spray a microfibre cloth with general-purpose spray and wipe the marks to remove them.

This is also a good time to clean your heater and air conditioner filters as per the manufacturer's instructions.

Light Fittings

DUST THE COVER OF THE LIGHT FITTING to remove as much dust as possible. If your cover is detachable, take it down and wash with warm soapy water to remove any dust and dead insects. Allow the fitting to dry completely before replacing. If your cover is not detachable, spray a microfibre cloth with general-purpose spray and wipe any marks to remove them.

Walls

CLEANING WALLS MIGHT BE THE LAST THING you would ever want to do! However undesirable it may seem, it's often necessary to remove handprints and smears. Freshly cleaned walls will brighten your whole room.

To clean your walls quickly and easily, you will need a flat mop (keep a separate pad for walls), white vinegar and water.

Pop some hot water in your mop bucket or laundry tub and add a good glug of vinegar. A 1:10 ratio of vinegar to water should do it, but there's no need to measure.

Wet your mop, wring until damp and then start on your walls. You can go up and down or left to right – whatever feels more comfortable. Refresh the water as you go, if necessary.

Once your walls are dry, assess any stubborn scuff marks, etc. Spray them with hairspray, hand sanitiser or isopropyl alcohol and rub with a microfibre cloth.

Spot-cleaning or cleaning without a mop

While a mop really does speed up the process and reduce physical effort, not everyone has a separate mop pad they are able to use. If this is the case for you, you might like to simply spot-clean your walls with a cloth, water and vinegar. Use the same 1:10 solution but instead of the mop head, use your cloth and just cover the areas that you need to clean or that you are comfortable accessing. Use a sturdy stepladder to avoid overreaching.

Skirting Boards
• • • • • • • • • • • • • • • • •

YOU MAY BE ABLE TO DO YOUR SKIRTING at the same time as your walls – it really depends on the profile of your skirting.

If you have decorative skirting, you may like to use a spin mop if you have one, or just pop a wet terry towelling nappy on the end of your mop and use that. If you are okay with bending or kneeling you can simply wipe skirting boards with a cloth.

To remove scuffs, hand sanitiser and hairspray do a great job on gloss and semi-gloss surfaces.

Windows

· · · · · · · · · · · · · · · · ·

USING THE GLASS AND STAINLESS STEEL CLEANER (see Cleaning Recipes), liberally spray the window and use a glass-cleaning cloth to wipe the whole surface, up and down. When doing the other side, use the same method but with left-to-right strokes. When the window dries, if there happens to be a streak you will immediately know which side it is on and can fix it quickly.

A lot of Mums Who members recommend the Kärcher Window Vac – it saves them time and energy when cleaning windows (and shower screens).

Window tracks

To clean the tracks of sliding windows, start by vacuuming out as much as you can using the crevice tool (the long, thin attachment) on your vacuum. If you can't get into the track with that, fit a cardboard tube over the end of the vacuum and pinch to size. If there is grime in the tracks, wrap the head of a flat-head screwdriver with a damp cloth and wipe out the track. If the surrounding area is appropriate you can even steam-clean with a handheld steam cleaner.

Flyscreens

For a general clean, use the soft brush attachment on your vacuum to remove any dust and debris.

To give your flyscreens a deep clean, remove them from the windows and place them flat onto grass or concrete. Use your garden hose to wet the screens thoroughly. Use the brush from your dustpan to brush warm soapy water over the screens. Ensure you wipe the frame and the mesh. Flip each screen over and repeat. Rinse the screens off with the hose, prop them up and allow them to dry fully before returning them to the windows.

If you can't remove your screens, you can use a vacuum with a brush attachment or a damp cloth to clean them.

Curtains *and* Blinds

· · · · · · · · · · · · · · · · ·

IT IS REALLY EASY TO FORGET about your window coverings, even though you use them every day! Keeping your curtains dust free and clean can improve the overall feel of your home and even reduce dust in the rest of your home.

There are lots of different types of curtains, blinds and fabrics. Here's how to clean some of the most common ones.

Blockout curtains

The blockout backing on curtains can make them hard to clean at home. Sometimes a washing machine can damage them beyond repair. Spot-cleaning with a damp cloth and some upholstery-safe spray cleaner is recommended to avoid damage. Spray the cloth (not the curtain) and wipe any marks you see. If you do this regularly the upkeep won't seem like hard work.

If you have a Bissell SpotClean machine, you can use it to do small sections, or even lay the curtain flat and complete the whole curtain.

A steam cleaner is another great tool for efficiency. Direct the steam onto the fabric side of the curtain, then use the suction hose to suck the moisture from the fabric. Avoid wetting the fabric as much as possible to cut down drying time, and to avoid water stains and mould.

Wipe the backing with a damp cloth, if required.

To keep the curtains dust free, use the soft brush attachment on your vacuum cleaner and go over both sides.

Sheer curtains

Not all sheer fabrics wash or even spot-clean well. Ensure you know your fabric before choosing how to clean these curtains.

If you have a robust sheer fabric, consider machine-washing the curtains in a front loader. Remove the curtains from the rod/track and fold them over your arm. Gently place the curtains in your front-loading washing machine (a top loader may wring the curtains too tightly) and wash on a delicates cycle, using your regular laundry detergent. Do *not* spin. When the cycle is finished, remove the curtains immediately and hang back onto the rod/track, in a closed position.

This method is *not* suitable for all fabrics.

Venetian blinds or shutters

These are the bane of our existence! Venetians look amazing but get dusty and grimy really quickly. Cleaning them can be laborious, especially in the kitchen where grease can be an issue. (If you have venetians in the kitchen, always turn your rangehood or exhaust fan on when cooking to help minimise grease deposits.)

Wiping each blade is really the best way to effectively clean venetians – especially if they are made of timber, which shouldn't be hosed. Use a cloth dampened with mildly soapy water, pinch cloth over each blade and run along the length, so that you're cleaning its top and bottom at the same time.

Bunnings sell dusters and cloths designed to dust multiple blades at once, which you may find helpful.

For plastic or metal venetians, some Mums Who members take them down and hose them outside. The pressure from your hose may damage your blinds but lots of members have great success and find the process much less tedious.

An alternative would be to hang your blinds against a hard surface like a fence. Wet a broom with soapy water and give them a gentle brush.

Fabric blinds

Most fabric blinds are spot-clean only. Check with the manufacturer as they may have specific recommendations. In most cases, water only is the best solution. Using a slightly damp, white cloth (to avoid dye transfer), wipe the marks until clean. Wipe in one direction only to avoid smudging. Some manufacturers recommend only using baby wipes, so it's best to check.

Allow to dry before opening the blind again.

Vinyl/plastic blinds

These types of blinds (shade screens, roller blinds, some vertical blinds) are probably the simplest window coverings to clean. Use a damp cloth to wipe the whole blind. Leave the blind down to dry before rolling it up.

Flooring

· · · · · · · · · · · · · · · ·

WHETHER YOU HAVE LEVEL FLOORING, stairs, sloping floors or a combination of these, the most important consideration for cleaning is the *type* of floor covering.

Carpeted floors

Carpet is a warm and inviting floor covering that many people choose to have in their living room and bedroom areas especially. Although comfortable, carpet requires regular upkeep to ensure it remains clean and fresh-smelling.

Shampooing

To shampoo your carpet well, you will need a carpet-cleaning machine of some sort. We recommend the Bissell ProHeat 2X Revolution

Pet. This is a great unit at a great price point. Its suction and agitation are far superior to the entry-level machines. The machine makes quick work of carpet stains, spills and general carpet cleaning. Use this machine as per the manufacturer's instructions and with the designated formula.

If you are using a carpet-cleaning machine, you simply need to fill the clean water tank with water and the recommended amount of formula (make sure to add the water before the formula, to avoid suds in the tank), then insert the tank into the machine. Ensure the waste water tank is attached, plug the machine in and go for it!

If you can't purchase a carpet cleaner of your own, there are various models available for hire from Bunnings and some supermarkets. You can purchase the correct formula from the place of hire.

Rachael's *tip*
If you can work quickly and split the hire cost with a friend, even better!

Spot stains

Most carpet stains are cleaned easily with an upholstery-cleaning machine. We like the Bissell SpotClean Turbo. These types of machines suck the spill right up, then the formula works to remove the stain.

If you have something a bit trickier, or you don't have an upholstery-cleaning machine, then try these tips:

- **SLIME:** Slime can dry very solidly on your carpet, clothing and furniture. To remove it, pour a good amount of white vinegar directly onto the slime. Agitate the slime with your fingers or a soft brush until it becomes flexible again. Start removing what you can with a scraper, soaking up the vinegar with an old towel as you go. Keep going until the slime is removed.

- **OLD GENERIC STAINS:** Old stains can be difficult to remove, even for professional carpet cleaners. Mums Who Clean members have had great success using a Polident solution (see Cleaning Recipes). Spray the mixture over the stain to wet but not soak the stain. Gently dab with a white cloth or old towel until the stain reduces. Repeat until the stain has been removed. Ensure you are soaking up the excess liquid as you go.

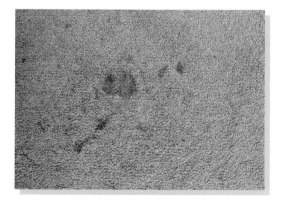

Tiled floors

For any type of tile, an all-in-one vacuum/mop (e.g. a CrossWave or HIZERO) will cut back on cleaning time and physical effort considerably. The cleaning method you choose will depend on your floor type and personal preferences.

Matt tiles

Depending on the material your tiles are made from and what kind of mess is on them, it may be better to use cold water – this is especially true for matt porcelain as it gives a nicer finish. Things tend to stick really hard to matt tiles, and a layer of grime can slowly build up over time.

To mop your matt floor tiles, mix $\frac{1}{2}$ cup of apple cider vinegar (or white vinegar if you prefer) and a dash of dishwashing liquid in a bucket of hot or cold water. The temperature will depend on whether your tiles are ceramic (hot water) or porcelain (cold water). The temperature isn't strictly essential so you can select one based on the finish you prefer. Use a wet but not dripping mop to clean your tiles and allow the tiles to dry fully before walking on them.

Unfortunately most matt tiles will need deep-cleaning about once a year on top of your regular mopping. To deep-clean your tiles, you can use a Polident solution (see Cleaning Recipes). Pour the solution all over the floor and move it around with a soft broom to cover the whole surface. You may need quite a bit of mixture depending on the size of the area. Leave the mixture for 10–20 minutes. If you have an all-in-one vacuum/mop (e.g. a CrossWave), you can use this to lift grime and the Polident mixture off the floor. You can also use a spin mop or another type of mop that is easy to wring. Or, if you are short on time or energy, this is a great time to employ a professional floor cleaner to do the job for you.

Gloss tiles

Vacuum your floor thoroughly before filling a bucket with hot water, a little white vinegar and a dash of dishwasher rinse aid. Use a damp mop to clean the tiles, ensuring they are thoroughly dry before walking on them. You will be left with a beautiful glossy finish.

If you have a build-up of product on your tiles, you might find they are left with footprints and other marks, even after they are dry. To remove this build-up, mix up a stronger vinegar and water solution and mop vigorously.

Slate

Start by vacuuming or sweeping your slate floors as normal. Add a generous squirt of pH-neutral dishwashing liquid to a bucket of hot water. Use a damp spin mop (this type is best, as it can get into the crevices of the uneven slate surface) to mop the slate thoroughly. Dry your slate thoroughly with a soft towel to avoid water stains.

Ensure you seal your slate regularly to prolong its life span and aid in cleaning.

If you drop something likely to stain the slate, immediately sprinkle bicarbonate of soda (bicarb) over the area to absorb it. This will hopefully prevent the stain completely or at least make it easier to remove. Once the spill is absorbed, sweep the bicarb up with a dustpan and brush.

To remove general stains, use the detergent mix described above and scrub the stain gently with a soft brush.

For more stubborn stains, you can use isopropyl alcohol combined with water (1:8 ratio of alcohol to water). Simply use the solution with a cloth to rub the stained area with as much force as required.

As an alternative to isopropyl alcohol, you can combine bicarb with a little water to form a paste. Coat the stain with the paste and let it dry fully. Wipe the mixture off the slate with a damp cloth and ensure the area is dry before walking on it.

As slate is a natural stone, you need to ensure you use safe products to clean the surface. Acidic, oil-based and abrasive cleaners should be avoided to prevent etching, stains or damage.

Grout

Work in sections of your floor that will take you approximately 10 minutes to clean. Spray or pour a grout-cleaning solution (see Cleaning Recipes) onto your grout. Leave the solution for 10 minutes to activate.

Before returning to scrub the first area, apply the solution to the next section of grout so that it can activate while you are scrubbing the first section. Once the activation time is up, use a grout brush to scrub each section of grout. Once you have finished scrubbing the grout, mop your flooring as normal.

Karlie's *tip*
You can buy long-handled grout brushes from Bunnings and commercial cleaning suppliers.

Once your grout is spotless, it's worth sealing it to make cleaning much easier in future. Sealing grout is very

Rachael's *tip*
To reduce effort, use a broom to apply the grout cleaner liberally.

simple – sort of like spraying hairspray. You can get sealant from Bunnings or any tile supply shop.

Natural timber floors

Start by removing the dust and debris from your floors by sweeping or vacuuming. If you find dust is an issue on your floors, you might like to get a dusting pad for your spray mop, if you have one. Rubbermaid and Koh both offer these options.

Once you've dusted, use a spray mop and a solution of white vinegar and hot or cold water depending on your preference (1:3 ratio of vinegar to water) to mop the floor. Use minimal liquid – just enough to keep your mop damp.

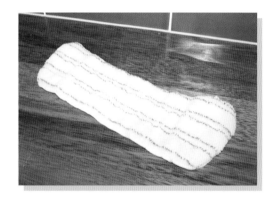

Do not use steam or steam mops on your timber floors. These can cause considerable damage as the steam can penetrate the timber and cause it to swell.

Laminate floors

Laminate flooring is not waterproof so you should be very careful and follow the directions from its manufacturer. Avoid applying lots of water or any steam. A slightly damp microfibre mop may be best for your laminate. To dampen the mop, spray lightly with a solution of water and vinegar (you can use the Glass and Stainless Steel Cleaner in the Cleaning Recipes chapter).

As with natural timber floors, if you have lots of dust settling, you might like to get a dusting pad for your mop.

Hybrid or vinyl flooring

A spray mop with a vinegar-and-water solution is a great way to clean hybrid or vinyl flooring. You don't need a lot of effort to clean these types of floors, so this method is perfect.

If your vinyl is fairly old or has grooves in it (such as faux wood grain), you may like to use a stiff broom and Polident solution (see Cleaning Recipes) to clean the floor every so often. This will get rid of the grime in those crevices. Work in small areas if possible and wipe up as you go.

Be sure to check your flooring is waterproof first. Some types are not.

Disinfecting

Disinfecting your home can be a great way to reduce the chance of illness spreading through it. You might like to give the house a once-over after someone in your family has been ill or as a precautionary measure at other times.

It may surprise you to hear that some common germs (various bacteria and viruses) can survive on surfaces in your home for many days. The length of time depends on lots of different factors, such as the type of surface, the type of germ and the environment. Government health websites are great resources for information on specific germs.

It is very important to note the difference between an antibacterial cleaning product and a true disinfectant – they are used differently and do different things. While antibacterial cleaning products help to physically remove dirt and germs, they may not completely kill bacteria, and (unless they claim antiviral properties) often don't work against viruses. In fact, many are only as effective as ordinary soaps, detergents, and warm water when it comes to eliminating bacteria.

Disinfectants, on the other hand, are designed to kill the germs they come into contact with. Disinfectants with antiviral properties will have this stated on their label. It's very important to clean the surface (you can use soap and water, or any multipurpose cleaner) before this step, as an unclean surface may disrupt the disinfection process. Different disinfectants have different dilution ratios, so be sure to check the packaging for product-specific information.

You might want to start by cleaning and disinfecting high-touch surfaces such as doorknobs, handles and light switches before progressing to other areas of your house. Note that disinfectants require time to be fully effective, so if the product doesn't specify a time, leave it on the surface for around ten minutes.

There are lots of products available that can make disinfecting your home easy. It's extremely important you use these products as directed to ensure the product does indeed disinfect the surface and to avoid causing damage to your property.

Bleach, when used as directed, is a very cheap way to disinfect. You should thoroughly clean the surface before using the diluted bleach method.

Prepare the bleach solution immediately before using it, if possible, and no more than 24 hours beforehand. Once it's made up, the shelf life is short.

Soak your cloth in the bleach solution and wipe over the surface. Remember that bleach is not safe for all surfaces and materials.

If you prefer, you can use 70-90% alcohol to disinfect. Clean the area first, soak a cloth in the alcohol solution and wipe over the area.

Ensure your home is well ventilated and that you take appropriate precautions, such as using gloves, a mask and safety glasses. Never combine bleach with other chemicals unless directed to by the bleach packaging.

entry

never be embarrassed to

open the door again

YOUR ENTRYWAY IS THE FIRST PART OF YOUR HOME that you and your visitors step into. Families often inject their personality into their entryway so they are always greeted with an area that makes them happy. Artwork, family photos, mirrors and decorative items are all commonly found in an engaging entry.

Decorative Items *and* Photo Frames

USE A DUSTER OR DUSTING CLOTH to remove all the dust from these items. If their materials are not porous, you can spray a dry microfibre cloth with a general-purpose spray to wipe them down thoroughly.

Mirrors

MIRRORED SURFACES can be cleaned using a general-purpose spray, or a solution of vinegar and water. Spray the surface and give it a wipe with a glass-cleaning cloth.

If your mirror has a decorative frame, take care not to damage the finish. You can use a paintbrush and a soft cloth to remove dust or debris that has gathered on the frame.

Artwork

· · · · · · · · · · · · · · · · ·

USUALLY ALL THAT IS NEEDED to clean artwork is a quick dust with a soft duster. If the artwork is behind glass, you can use a dry screen-cleaning cloth to wipe it down. This will prevent any cleaning products from damaging your artwork.

If your piece has a frame, you can clean it in the same way as a mirror frame, as described previously.

Take care to avoid using any harsh or abrasive cleaners on artwork, as they may ruin the work.

Rachael's *tip*

If you have a gallery wall or lots of hung frames, use a dab of Blu Tack or similar on the back of each one so that the frames don't move when dusting.

Furniture

· · · · · · · · · · · · · · · ·

REMOVE DUST WITH A DUSTER OR DUSTING CLOTH. Spray furniture items with a general-purpose spray and wipe over each part with a microfibre cloth.

Doormat

· · · · · · · · · · · · · · · ·

MOST OF THE TIME, A GOOD SHAKE IS SUFFICIENT to remove the stuck-in debris from a doormat. Depending on what your mat is made of, you may also like to give it a quick vacuum.

If you use a carpet mat, you can shampoo it when you do the rest of your carpets.

kitchen

keep the heart of your
home ticking with these
easy-to-follow tips

CLEANING YOUR KITCHEN CAN SEEM LIKE an intimidating task. It's the place where a lot of mess occurs, and it occurs every day. Making breakfast, lunch and dinner is a messy business, and kids grabbing snacks can add to the chaos.

Here we will share with you easy ways to give your kitchen a thorough clean and maintain it with as little effort as possible.

Start with the parts of the kitchen listed in the General Cleaning chapter. When you have finished these, it is time to move on to cleaning more specific areas.

Cabinets *and* Drawers

· · · · · · · · · · · · · · ·

CLEAR A SPACE ON YOUR BENCHTOP or dining table where you can place items from your cabinets and drawers. Select one cabinet or drawer and remove all the items. Vacuum or sweep out any crumbs and wipe every surface. You can do this using a microfibre cloth with vinegar and water, or with a general-purpose cleaner such as Koh Universal Cleaner or TRUEECO Everyday Cleaner. Don't forget to clean your organising trays and baskets as you go.

Kickboards

· · · · · · · · · · · · · · ·

TO CLEAN YOUR KICKBOARDS, spray the surface with a general-purpose spray and then wipe with a microfibre cloth to remove any marks. For stubborn marks, use some hairspray on a microfibre cloth and give the marks a quick scrub.

Pantry

YOU CAN CLEAN YOUR PANTRY one shelf at a time or you can empty it all at once, depending on your preference. When you have everything out, this is a great time to go through your products, remove anything that is not needed and check use-by dates. Pantries can quickly become a mess and out-of-date items can start to pile up.

Clean your pantry shelving in the same way as your kitchen cabinets.

Look at the items from your pantry. Group each one with similar products before putting them back into the pantry. This will help you keep track of your products and prevent the pantry from becoming a mess again.

Fridge *and* Freezer

IT'S EASIEST TO REMOVE ALL ITEMS from your fridge or freezer at the same time, and clean in one go. If you have sensitive items in your fridge, though, you may prefer to clean shelf by shelf.

Using a microfibre cloth with vinegar and water, soapy water or a general-purpose spray, wipe all the walls, shelving and drawers in your fridge or freezer. To remove a large spill or more stubborn marks, create a paste with bicarb and water, dip a cleaning toothbrush into the paste and scrub the affected area until it's clean. Wipe the remaining paste away with your cloth.

Check the expiry dates of all items before returning them to the fridge or freezer. Wipe the food packaging too, to clean up any spills or leaks.

Wipe down the outside of your fridge, including the water or ice dispenser, with a product suitable for the type of surface you have. A general-purpose spray like Koh Universal Cleaner is suitable for most materials.

If you are having issues with a bad odour in your fridge, placing a box or bowl of bicarb in the back of the fridge can help to absorb it. Replace the bicarb each time you clean your fridge.

For regular maintenance of your newly cleaned fridge, do a quick sort and clear-out before each grocery shop.

Karlie's *tip*

You can use the old bicarb from your fridge to clean other areas of your home such as your sink, dishwasher (see below) or washing machine (see the Laundry chapter).

Dishwasher

A DISHWASHER IS GENERALLY USED at least once a day, so it's a good idea to clean yours regularly to avoid build-up of food residue and stale water.

Start with cleaning the seal on the machine door by wiping with a damp cloth or vinegar. Using the same cloth, wipe along the bottom of the door – there may be a lot of build-up. (This can be done regularly, each time you load or unload.)

Check the filter for any food residue and remove it, following the instructions in your appliance manual (every dishwasher is different).

Check the spray arms for residue and carefully wipe with a microfibre cloth. If this doesn't remove the build-up, check your manual for instructions on how to remove the spray arms for cleaning.

The racks and cutlery tray can get food caught in them so make sure that you check these and give them a wipe.

You can clean your dishwasher with bicarb and vinegar. There is no exact recipe – just go with what works for you – but a good guide is approximately 1 cup of bicarb to 2 cups of vinegar. Sprinkle the bicarb over the base of the machine, then pour the vinegar over it. The bicarb and vinegar will react and fizz. Once the fizz reaction subsides run a cycle on the hottest setting to help loosen any residue or build-up in the machine.

To keep the outside of the dishwasher clean, wipe it with a microfibre cloth, using a general-purpose spray or stainless steel cleaner.

Microwave
. . . .

MICROWAVES CAN GET DIRTY – QUICKLY. Heating up foods and liquids can cause them to splatter, leaving mess all over the inside of your microwave.

The easiest way to keep a microwave clean is to give it a quick wipe with a damp cloth after each use. However, this doesn't always happen, and spills that dry may leave a residue that is hard to remove. Mix up a solution of vinegar and warm water and, using a spray bottle or a cloth, let some of the solution sit on tougher spills to soften them. After a few minutes, wipe with the cloth. You can use the vinegar and water to wipe down the outside of your microwave too, or use a general-purpose spray.

To speed up your cleaning you might like to microwave a cup of water or vinegar with some lemon slices in it before you begin. Microwave time will depend on your settings. The solution should create a steam that can help to soften any residue and make it easier to wipe away.

Rangehood

· · · · · · · · · · · · · · · · ·

RANGEHOODS ARE ONE OF THE MOST IMPORTANT appliances in the kitchen. Not only do they remove smoke, steam and fumes, they also help to make cleaning the kitchen much easier. As it sucks up the air, the rangehood also sucks up grease and grime, which is trapped in the filters.

There are several ways to clean your filters and how you do it will depend on the type of material the filters are made from. Be aware that some methods will tarnish or ruin certain materials, so be sure to consult the rangehood's instruction manual first.

Dishwasher

The dishwasher is a great way to clean rangehood filters – they go in greasy and come out sparkling clean. But you need to be careful using this method as some materials can discolour, turning yellow or black.

Dishwashing liquid

Fill your kitchen sink with very hot water and dishwashing liquid. Add the filters and leave to soak. When the water has cooled down enough for you to touch it comfortably, give the filters a scrub with a non-scratch sponge or dish brush. Remove from water and leave to dry thoroughly before returning to the rangehood.

Dishwasher tablets

Fill your kitchen sink with hot water and 2 dishwasher tablets. Add the filters and leave to soak overnight. The next day, give the filters a scrub with a non-scratch sponge or dish brush. Remove and leave to dry thoroughly before returning to the rangehood.

Bicarb

Fill your kitchen sink with boiling water and ½ cup bicarb. Add the filters and leave to soak. Give the filters a scrub with a non-scratch sponge or dish brush. Remove and leave to dry thoroughly before returning to the rangehood.

Steam cleaner

If you have a steam cleaner, this is an easy way to remove the grease from your rangehood filters. Place your filters on an old towel, or in your sink if it is large enough (or a large container or bath, if not). Using the smallest attachment for the steam cleaner nozzle, spray the filter to remove the grease. Rinse under hot water and dry thoroughly before returning to the rangehood.

Cooktop
· · · · · · · · · · · · · · · · ·

SPILLS, SPLATS AND SPITS ARE COMMON on a cooktop. If they are not cleaned quickly they can harden, making them difficult to remove. Obviously the best way to deal with this is to clean your cooktop after each use, but that isn't always possible. There are many cleaning products on the market that you can use on your cooktop, depending on its surface type. Ensure all cooktop surfaces are completely cool before beginning.

Gas

General-purpose sprays (e.g. Koh Universal Cleaner and TRUEECO Everyday Cleaner) are easy to use and leave the cooktop surface looking great. Our Glass and Stainless Steel Cleaner (see Cleaning Recipes) can also be used to clean stainless steel surfaces. For spots that are harder to remove, cover the spill with some of your cleaning product and allow it to soften before wiping away.

Burners

Gas cooktop burners are made from a variety of materials. Check your instruction manual to find out what the burners are made of, and follow the instructions for cleaning. The safest cleaning method is hot soapy water and a scrubbing brush. Some materials are dishwasher safe but others will tarnish, so it's best to avoid the dishwasher method if you're not sure. Avoid using harsh cleaners such as oven cleaners or laundry soakers (e.g. Napisan).

Grates and trivets

The grates and trivets that your pots sit on can be quite heavy and awkwardly shaped. Many Mums Who Clean members find it easiest to pop these in the dishwasher. If you don't have a dishwasher or your grates won't fit, soak them in your sink, laundry trough or a large container with some soapy water. For areas of build-up, use a damp magic eraser to remove them.

Ceramic, glass and induction

The easiest way to clean these types of cooktops is to use warm soapy water and a soft sponge or cloth. Wipe over any spills to remove them. If you are having difficulty, moisten problem spots with the soapy water and leave for a few minutes to soften, then wipe with your cloth.

If you have heavy and stubborn scratch-type marks, you may want to consider using a commercial product (e.g. Cerapol Ceramic Glass & Induction Cooktop Cleaner), and a cooktop scraper tool made specifically for the purpose.

Coil

The easiest way to clean an electric coil cooktop is to remove the coils (if you are unsure how to do this, consult the instruction manual for your cooktop) and wash them in warm soapy water, taking care not to wet any electrical connections. If you have stubborn stains, you can use a paste made from bicarb and water. Cover the coil with the paste and leave for 15–20 minutes. Then, using a scrubbing brush, remove the paste and rinse with warm water. Put the coils aside to dry.

Using the warm soapy water, wipe the drip tray to remove any marks.

You can also use a spray made from vinegar and water to clean this type of cooktop.

Solid plate

Use a plastic scraper to remove any debris, taking care not to damage the surface of the hotplates. Using a general-purpose or stovetop cleaner, mist each plate then rub with a sponge to remove any marks. Fill a small bucket with warm water and wipe over each plate with a damp cloth, changing the cloth as required. Wipe away the water with a clean cloth as you go, and ensure each plate is completely dry when finished to avoid rusting. Consider using covers to protect the plates between uses.

Oven

OVENS ARE THE HARDEST PART OF A KITCHEN to keep clean. Something always spills and bakes onto the shelves or the base, leaving a horrible mess to clean up. Wiping out your oven regularly helps make it easier to clean. However, if you have some hard-to-remove build-up, there are a few ways to deal with it.

Dishwasher tablets

Fill your sink, bathtub or a large container with hot water. Remove your oven racks and loosely wrap each one in aluminium foil. Pop an old towel onto the bottom of your bath to protect it. Place the foil-wrapped rack into the bath. (The foil does not need to fully enclose the rack.) Place the rest of your racks on top – and don't forget the shelf rails, which detach from the side of the oven. (Don't put the drip trays in.)

Place one dishwasher tablet per rack into the bath. Cover with hot water and soak until the water is cold. Drain the water and discard the foil. Give each rack/rail a quick wipe down with a cloth or a soapy steel-wool pad. You will be amazed at how easily the build-up on the racks just wipes away.

You can also use a dishwasher tablet to help clean the rest of your oven. Fill a bowl or jug with some warm water. Wearing thick rubber gloves to protect your hands, dip a tablet into the water and then rub it all over the inside surfaces of your oven. Leave for a few minutes. Spray with warm water and wipe clean with a microfibre cloth.

Koh Universal Cleaner

This is a great general-purpose spray and it is a good product to use to clean your oven. Remove your oven racks and shelf rails and pop them on some towels. Give them a good spray with Koh and leave for a few minutes. Wipe over with a warm, damp wet cloth. If your racks have stubborn marks, brush them over with a Koh Diamond Sponge, dampened with the Universal Cleaner solution. For the surfaces inside your oven, use the same method but ensure you conduct a scratch test first, as per Koh's recommendation.

Splashback

· · · · · · · · · · · · · · · · · ·

Tile

Spray the splashback surface with a general-purpose spray and use a microfibre cloth to wipe the whole area vigorously. If the grout has any splash marks, use a wet magic eraser block to wipe over and remove them.

Mirror/glass/acrylic/stainless steel

Use a general-purpose spray and a glass-cleaning cloth to remove any marks. If there are stubborn marks, spray with the general-purpose spray and leave to soften before wiping off.

Engineered stone

Wipe over the splashback regularly with a damp cloth and soapy water.

Granite

A microfibre cloth, warm water and a small amount of dishwashing liquid are all that is needed for daily cleaning. A general-purpose spray can also be used.

If your granite is black or a similar dark colour, you may find streak marks a challenge to deal with. To avoid the streaks, clean with a dry cloth and a general-purpose spray that is safe to use on stone.

Marble

Clean on a daily basis with warm water and a microfibre cloth. A pH-neutral dishwashing liquid can also be used and is helpful for marks and stains.

Window

Use a glass cleaner to clean the glass sections, as you would for a normal window. Ensure you use a general-purpose spray to wipe the windowsill and remove any greasy build-up.

Benchtops

· · · · · · · · · · · · · · · · ·

KITCHEN BENCHTOPS COME IN A RANGE of materials, and cleaning each material requires a specific method.

Begin by clearing all your items off the benchtop.

Engineered stone

This is one of the most common benchtop materials. It is a non-porous surface that is very durable, easy to clean, and difficult to stain or scratch.

The easiest way to keep stone clean is to wipe it down regularly with a damp cloth and soapy water.

Do not use your normal dishcloth, as this may have residue from your dishes that can discolour or stain your benchtop.

Use a chopping board or heatproof mat to protect your benchtop. Soak up any spills immediately – don't wait.

If something does stain your benchtop, do not use abrasive tools to clean it. Steel wool and scourers can damage the surface. Using a commercial stone cleaner on a damp cloth is the safest way to remove stains from your engineered stone.

Laminate

This is another common benchtop material that is resistant to staining and easy to keep clean. However, it is also easy to scratch, and it can burn.

Wipe away spills and marks with a damp cloth or a general-purpose cleaner. Rubbing gently with a clean, dry cloth brings back the brightness to laminate surfaces.

If something does stain your benchtop, do not use abrasive tools. Steel wool and scourers may damage your surface. Make a paste with bicarb and water and gently rub into the affected area, then wipe clean with a damp cloth.

Timber

Timber benchtops need more maintenance than some other surfaces to keep them looking good. Sanding and sealing, or oiling, needs to be done regularly – depending on how your timber was originally sealed – to keep the benchtop looking fresh.

Clean your timber benchtop regularly with dishwashing liquid and a damp microfibre cloth or a general-purpose spray. This will keep it clean and minimise staining. To remove stubborn stains, use a mixture of lemon juice and salt to gently wipe over the area. Wipe the residue up with a clean, damp cloth.

Wooden benchtops can distort when exposed to water too often or when spills are left for long periods. Clean up spills as soon as they happen.

Stainless steel

Stainless steel is an extremely durable surface. It is heat resistant, hard to scratch and easy to keep looking great.

For daily maintenance, use a microfibre cloth dampened with a solution of dishwashing liquid and warm water, or a general-purpose spray. Our Glass and Stainless Steel Cleaner recipe (see Cleaning Recipes) can also be used.

For stains, a combination of bicarb and vinegar can be used. Sprinkle bicarb onto the stain and tip a little vinegar over for the fizz reaction, before gently scrubbing with a clean cloth.

Polished concrete

Maintaining a concrete benchtop is similar to maintaining an engineered stone surface, although concrete benchtops require sealing.

Clean up spills as they happen using a soft, damp cloth. A general-purpose spray is also helpful. Make sure that your products are pH-neutral.

Avoid any type of citrus coming into contact with the concrete benchtop, as acid can corrode some concrete surfaces.

Marble

Marble is very porous and can stain easily. It needs to be sealed regularly.

Clean daily with warm water and a microfibre cloth. A pH-neutral dishwashing liquid is helpful for marks and stains.

Do not use low-pH/acidic cleaners such as citrus juice or vinegar on marble – they can corrode the surface (called 'etching').

Granite

Granite is a very durable natural stone that is easy to clean.

A microfibre cloth, warm water and a small amount of dishwashing liquid are all that is needed for daily cleaning. A general-purpose spray that is safe for stone can also be used.

If your granite is black or a similar dark colour, you may find streak marks a challenge to deal with. To avoid these, clean with a dry cloth and a general-purpose spray that is safe for stone.

Porcelain

Porcelain is very resistant to stains and scratches and can handle high heat. It can be maintained in a similar way to engineered stone.

Wiping down regularly with a cloth dampened in soapy water is great for daily maintenance.

Even though porcelain is heat resistant, it's best to use a chopping board or heatproof mat to protect your benchtop. Soak up any spills immediately – don't wait.

If something does stain your benchtop, do not use abrasive tools. Steel wool and scourers may damage the surface. A paste of warm water and bicarb will remove most stains.

Sink

• • • • • • • • • • • • • • • •

USING A DISHWAND OR SPONGE, wipe any debris into the sink strainer – use a little water to help, if required. Remove the strainer and discard the scraps. Do not return the strainer to the plughole.

Fill your kettle and boil. Sprinkle bicarb over the sink and plughole, then spray or tip white vinegar over the bicarb to create a fizz reaction. Slowly pour the boiling water from your kettle over the remaining bicarb, and a good amount down the plughole – this will clean your drain and ensure that the bicarb doesn't harden.

You can pop the sink strainer into the dishwasher to get it nice and clean. If you don't have a dishwasher, give it a wipe with dishwashing liquid and a scourer.

Use your dishwand or sponge to go over the sink surface once more, then dry with a tea towel or dry cloth.

Kettle

· · · · · · · · · · · · · · · · · ·

THE INSIDE OF YOUR KETTLE can get a build-up of limescale very quickly. There are some good products that can be purchased from the supermarket, such as Dr. Beckmann Appliance Descaler, but there are also some great natural products you can use that are better for the environment – and cost less, too.

Lemon

Slice or quarter a fresh lemon and place 1 or 2 pieces into the kettle. Fill the kettle with water, bring to the boil and leave to cool.

Once cool, pour out the water and discard the lemon. If required, give the inside a quick wipe with a cloth, or with a bottle brush if you have one. (A bottle brush is much easier to use for this.) Fill your kettle with fresh water and boil again. Discard the water and your kettle is good to go.

Vinegar

Vinegar is an amazing product with so many cleaning uses. One of those is cleaning your kettle.

Pour 1 cup of water into your kettle, followed by ¼ cup of white vinegar. (If your kettle has a lot of scale, you can increase to ½ cup of vinegar.) Leave this to sit for a few hours.

Discard the water and give your kettle a wipe. Boil some fresh water, then pour it out. Your kettle should now be sparkling clean and ready for your next cuppa.

Rachael's *tip*

Use the boiling water on garden weeds to eradicate them.

Toaster

· · · · · · · · · · · · · · · · ·

COLLECTING CRUMBS FROM A TOASTER is a major pain. Cleaning the toaster after each use is the best way to keep crumbs at bay. Most toasters have a little tray at the bottom that gathers crumbs. Remove this tray and pour the crumbs into the bin. However, often there are crumbs left in the toaster along the side that you just can't reach. Tipping your toaster upside down will remove the crumbs that didn't make it to the tray.

Karlie's *tip*

If the crumbs in your toaster are just not moving, use a hair dryer on a cool setting and give the inside of your toaster a little blast. This will help to loosen the stubborn crumbs.

Knife Block

KNIFE BLOCKS OFTEN SIT OUT IN THE OPEN, on the benchtop or a shelf, where they are susceptible to grease and grime. They can become dirty very quickly.

Cleaning a knife block begins with the knives. Take the knives from the block and give each one a good clean. Dry each knife and set aside.

To clean the block itself, turn it upside down and shake or tap to dislodge as much dust and debris as possible.

As the knife holes are quite deep, often a vacuum is not powerful enough to suck the dust out. Use a hair dryer to blow as many of the crumbs as possible loose and give the block another shake. Then use a vacuum to suck up as much of the dust as possible.

The outside of a knife block is easy to clean – just give it a wipe with a microfibre cloth and a general-purpose spray.

Tea Towels

TEA TOWELS ARE SOME OF THE MOST FREQUENTLY used towels in the home. You can clean them using your washing machine on a normal cycle. If this isn't enough, you can use the following methods to deep-clean your tea towels.

Boiling

Place your tea towels in a large cooking pot and cover with water. Place over high heat until the water is boiling. Agitate the towels with a large spoon and watch as the tea towels release the grime that has built up. You can also add some bicarb to the water for an extra boost.

Hot soaking

Prepare a bucket or tub of very hot water. Add a good glug of white vinegar, a rough ½ cup of bicarb and 2 scoops of washing powder (or the equivalent in laundry liquid). Leave for a few hours and then pop through your normal washing machine cycle.

Sponges

· · · · · · · · · · · · · · ·

THERE ARE MANY TYPES OF KITCHEN SPONGES. Reusable sponges are great for the environment and easy to keep clean. At the end of the night, you can pop them in the dishwasher for a quick clean. At the end of the week, include them in a normal washing machine cycle.

You can also wash your sponge in the sink, saturate with water and pop it in the microwave on high for one minute to sterilise. (Ensure that your sponge does not contain any metal before you do this.)

Stainless Steel Appliances

CARING FOR STAINLESS STEEL APPLIANCES is relatively easy. Most have a protective film on them, but if this is damaged, the stainless steel underneath is at risk. Caring for the surface from the beginning is important.

Remove marks with a solution of dishwashing liquid and water with a microfibre cloth. Follow the grain when wiping or polishing the appliance – this runs either horizontally or vertically. Rubbing in the same direction will give extra shine and keep your appliance looking good. A general-purpose spray like Koh is also a handy tool. Our recipe for Glass and Stainless Steel Cleaner (see Cleaning Recipes) can also be used.

Do not use steel wool, steel brushes or abrasive scrubbing pads/cloths. If using abrasive cleaning products make sure that they are stainless steel safe.

Cast Iron Pots *and* Pans

CAST IRON IS AN AMAZING COOKING TOOL. Its heat retention and non-stick properties, along with its durability, make it a very popular material for stovetop pots and pans. It is also easy to care for and keep clean if treated properly.

While still warm, use a paper towel or a cloth to remove any excess food or oil. Rinse with hot water and scrub with a non-abrasive pad. You can also use dishwashing liquid but make sure you rinse thoroughly to remove it.

Dry the surface completely, then heat over medium heat. Lightly coat the surface with oil and continue to wipe until all oils have been absorbed.

Let the pan cool completely before putting it away.

dining/
meals
area

alleviate the stress around

the hectic dinner rush

ALTHOUGH THE DINING ROOM OFTEN HAS very little in terms of furniture and decorations, it can be challenging to keep on top of, especially if you have young kids.

If your family makes a mess when they eat meals, the best course of action is to clean the mess right away. Some foods will stick really hard to the table or floor if left too long.

Wipe the table and the hard surfaces of chairs with a cloth and general-purpose spray, then pick up any food chunks from the floor and discard. Run a spray mop over the floor area (or vacuum the rug or carpet). This should take less than 5 minutes all up, and your space will always remain pretty clean. An all-in-one vacuum/mop (e.g. a CrossWave or HIZERO) can make clean-up even quicker on hard floors and rugs, as the food scraps won't need to be picked up first.

When you place hot serving bowls or plates on your dining table, be sure to use heatproof mats to prevent damage. Hot items placed directly on timber can leave white heat marks, which are troublesome to remove. Glass tables may scratch or shatter.

Dining Table
• • • • • • • • • • • • • • • •

USING A TABLECLOTH AND WASHING IT when required is a great way to make cleaning easy for your family. You can easily tip food scraps into the bin, then wash the tablecloth in the washing machine as needed.

If you don't use a tablecloth, clear the table fully after each meal. Wipe the food scraps into your hand and discard. Use an appropriate general-purpose cleaner for your table's surface, wiping over the full area. Replace any centrepiece you have once the surface is dry.

Timber

Most cleaning products are safe for timber but some can build up and cause the surface to become sticky over time. Ensure the product you are using is timber safe before applying. Options include Koh; a combination of vinegar, water and dishwashing liquid; and plain water. Spray your chosen solution on and wipe off immediately with a microfibre cloth.

Timber tabletops are susceptible to heat. Using a heatproof mat is beneficial for avoiding white heat marks. If you do accidentally get a heat mark, place a damp tea towel over the affected area and apply an iron, on a medium-heat steam setting, directly on the towel. Move in a circular motion for approximately 20–30 seconds, check the timber surface and repeat until the mark is gone. It may sound strange but the combination of the heat and the damp towel will actually draw the heat mark out of the timber.

If you accidentally scratch your timber dining table, you can rub a walnut kernel over the area – this will help to lessen the appearance of the scratch.

Glass

Glass tabletops often need a little more effort as you need to ensure both sides of the tabletop are shiny and clear. It's best to work with a dry glass-cleaning cloth and an appropriate cleaner. Koh Universal Cleaner works amazingly on glass surfaces as it doesn't soap up or leave a residue. The Koh Glass Cloth is a great accompaniment.

Concrete

Mild soapy water is best for concrete surfaces. Simply wet a cloth in the solution, wring well and wipe over the table.

You can also purchase cleaners specifically made for your concrete surface. Your manufacturer may have specific instructions for cleaning – it's best to check.

Chairs

DINING CHAIRS ARE MADE USING a wide variety of materials. The method you use to clean them will depend on the material.

Timber

Timber chairs can be cleaned as per a timber tabletop (see Dining Table section). It's best to attend to them after every meal to avoid any spilled food sticking to their surfaces.

Upholstered

Upholstered dining chairs can get gross really fast. Spot-cleaning them with a damp cloth and upholstery cleaner after every use is an efficient way to keep them looking schmick. Members of the Mums Who Clean Facebook group often use the Polident solution (see Cleaning Recipes) for lifting stains. Simply spray the upholstered areas and use a clean, dry cloth to work the stain from the fabric. Dab the area so it's as dry as possible to avoid a water mark.

If your fabric is delicate, you may like to spray the solution onto your cloth and then wipe it.

Metal, wire or plastic

You can clean your metal, wire or plastic chairs with any general-purpose cleaner. Spray a dry cloth with your chosen solution. Use the cloth to wipe over the chair's surface – don't forget the legs.

Karlie's *tip*

If you use felt floor-protector pads on the feet of your chairs, run a lint roller over them to remove all fluff, pet hair, dirt and dust. It's easiest to do this when you pop the chair up to mop the floor.

Highchair/Booster Straps

· · · · · · · · · · · · · · · ·

REMOVE FOOD SCRAPS FROM THE SEAT and wipe over the seat with a general-purpose cleaner.

Most highchair straps are removable and can be cleaned in your washing machine. Place the straps into a mesh laundry bag and wash with your regular washing.

If the straps are not removable, you can clean them while they are attached to the chair. Take a small bucket of water and dissolve some laundry soaker powder (such as Napisan) in it. Place the straps in the bucket, then scrub with a nailbrush or similar. Remove the straps from the solution and dry thoroughly with a towel.

If you have a plastic highchair, such as the IKEA ANTILOP, you can hose the chair down in the backyard or shower and leave it to dry.

Buffet/Sideboard

· · · · · · · · · · · · · · · ·

YOU CAN WIPE YOUR BUFFET OVER with a general-purpose spray and a microfibre cloth. Every now and then, remove the contents of the buffet and wipe them with a general-purpose spray if appropriate. Often buffets are used to store servingware that is not used very often, so quite a lot of dust can build up.

If your buffet has glass windows, use a glass cleaner and a glass-cleaning cloth to ensure the panes are streak free on both sides.

Centrepiece

CLEANING A TABLE CENTREPIECE DEPENDS on what type of item it is. The basic cleaning task is to remove the dust from the item.

Artificial Plants *and* Flowers

IF YOUR FLOWERS ARE VERY DUSTY, use a vacuum with a fine, soft brush attachment to remove as much dust as possible. Then use a damp cloth to wipe the leaves and petals well, removing the remaining dust and any spills.

For more robust artificial plants such as cacti, you can simply swish the plant in warm water to remove any dust and spills. Take care to not wet any areas that have adhesive.

Artwork

USE A DUSTER TO REMOVE ANY DUST from the artwork. This is usually all that is required to keep your piece clean. If the artwork is behind glass, you can use a dry screen-cleaning cloth to wipe any finger smudges from the glass.

Avoid using any harsh or abrasive cleaners on art as the piece may be ruined.

lounge
room

show some love to this
well-used part of your home

THE LOUNGE ROOM IS THE PLACE where your family relaxes and spends time together. The last thing you want to do is sit down in a big mess and be reminded of the jobs you need to get done.

Fabric Couch *and* Occasional Chairs

· · · · · · · · · · · · · · · · · ·

THESE ARE PROBABLY THE MOST USED ITEMS in a lounge room. No matter how careful you are, the kids' dirty hands, accidental spills, and pets will tend to leave marks on your fabric. There are a number of ways to remove these marks.

You can hire a professional to come and clean your couch for you. Most carpet-cleaning companies do this. However, this can be expensive if you want to do it regularly to keep your couch looking great.

The easiest and most cost-effective way to do it yourself is with a machine specifically for this purpose. There are lots of models available. Mums Who Clean members often recommend the Bissell SpotClean series.

Bissell SpotClean and SpotClean Turbo

These are great appliances if you just want to clean your couch or a small surface. (You can also clean carpets with them but it takes much longer as they only have a small head attachment.) If you do need to do a quick spot-clean, do the whole cushion that has the mark on it. If you don't, you will be left with a water mark that will be almost as ugly as the original stain.

Start by clearing off your couch and giving it a vacuum. Fill the clean tank of the SpotClean with warm water and the appropriate cleaning solution. Use the upholstery tool to spray all over your couch with the solution, spraying extra solution on any stains you need to remove. Let this sit for a few minutes, then use the tool to scrub the couch. Apply pressure to allow the machine to suck up the dirty fluid.

Once you have done this all over the couch, you will need to leave it for several hours to dry – preferably overnight. The next day you will have an amazing-looking couch.

Bissell ProHeat 2X Revolution Pet

Like the SpotClean, this machine is an excellent tool for cleaning upholstered items such as couches, bedheads, occasional chairs and dining chairs. The added benefit of the ProHeat is that it also does carpets and rugs, which is fantastic. The method is essentially the same as for the SpotClean; however, you need to attach the upholstery hose to the base of the machine first (see your instruction manual for specifics).

Polident solution

Many Mums Who Clean members use Polident solution to clean different areas of their homes (see Cleaning Recipes). The couch is one of these areas.

Spray Polident solution over the couch surface and scrub with a microfibre cloth. Leave to dry thoroughly.

If you have delicate fabric you may like to spray the solution onto your cloth before applying it to the fabric.

Upholstery cleaner

There are many upholstery products on the market and most work in the same way – by spraying, then using a cloth to work the product in and remove the stain.

A great, versatile commercial cleaner is Dr. Beckmann Carpet Stain Remover. The bottle has the scrubbing brush attached, making it really easy to grab for quick cleans.

Karlie's *tip*

A lint roller or dampened rubber cleaning glove can be run across carpets, furniture and surfaces to collect animal hair with ease. This prevents animal hair from blocking your vacuum cleaner.

Leather Couch *and* Occasional Chairs

• • • • • • • • • • • • • • •

WIPE YOUR COUCH WITH A MICROFIBRE CLOTH and a mild soap such as Lux Flakes or Sunlight Soap. Dry your couch thoroughly to ensure no water spots appear.

Apply a leather conditioner to a soft lint-free cloth. Work in a circular motion over one section of leather at a time. Once complete, use a soft, dry cloth to buff the surface. If you have not used leather conditioner on your couch before, do a small patch test to ensure it is suitable.

Some manufacturers have specific cleaning instructions. Please check these before cleaning your couch to ensure you don't void the warranty.

Rugs

· · · · · · · · · · · · · · · ·

HOW YOU CLEAN YOUR RUGS WILL DEPEND on what they are made of. Always check the manufacturer's recommendations. The Bissell machines mentioned earlier for couch cleaning are perfect for cleaning rugs, removing dirt and stains easily.

Some smaller rugs can be put in the washing machine or handwashed in a bathtub or shower. Some rugs can be cleaned outside with a pressure washer and hung to dry. Once wet, the rug will be very heavy so try to wash it in the location where you will be drying it.

If you don't have a pressure washer you can use laundry detergent, warm water and a broom. Work the solution in with a broom and then rinse with clean water. If your rug is delicate, ensure that your broom is soft and will not pull at the fibres.

Scrubbing with a clean cloth and an upholstery-safe cleaner is also an effective method for spot cleaning.

Television

· · · · · · · · · · · · · · · ·

FLAT SCREEN TVS ARE PRONE TO SCRATCHES and damage during cleaning. It is important to be careful when cleaning them.

As with all appliances and electrical devices, check the instruction manual for the manufacturer's recommendations.

Never clean your TV while it is turned on. This can cause damage to the screen. It is also much easier to see marks when the TV is turned off.

Dust the screen and outer edging first. A microfibre cloth or a wool duster are great options to remove dust from your TV.

To clean the screen, use a microfibre cloth lightly dampened with water, then dry with a different microfibre cloth. A TV-cleaning cloth (such as the White Magic Eco Cloth Screen & Lens) is a great alternative if the manufacturer suggests that you should not use liquids. To use these cloths, simply wipe the surface to remove the marks.

Do not use window cleaner, glass cleaner, soap or chemicals as these can damage the screen.

Electronics

ELECTRICAL APPLIANCES SUCH AS GAMING CONSOLES can gather a lot of dust. The instruction manual will have instructions on how to clean the device, but here are some other tips to make the job easier:

- A small, soft paintbrush is a great item to have on hand for cleaning electronic devices. Give the device a quick brush all over.
- Give the device a quick vacuum using a soft brush attachment.
- Once all dust is removed, wipe the device over with a microfibre cloth to finish it off.

Lamps

LAMPS ARE EXTREMELY EASY TO CLEAN once you discover the best tools to use. Many people use a vacuum with a soft brush attachment to vacuum the dust off the shade.

If you find your vacuum isn't getting all the dust, an effective and quick alternative is to

use a lint roller. Just roll the sticky lint roller over the surface of the shade to remove dust.

If you have marks on your shade you can use a general-purpose cleaning spray applied to a cloth and gently rub the area.

You can also clean any ceramic or glass components with the general-purpose spray and cloth.

Cushions
· · · · · · · · · · · · · · · · ·

YOU MAY THINK THAT DECORATIVE CUSHIONS don't get dirty too often, but surprisingly they can get quite dusty and grimy.

Hopefully you have chosen cushions that have removable covers – just throw them in the wash!

If not, you can clean cushions using the same methods you use for cleaning your couch. Make sure the cushions are dried thoroughly, on a flat surface, before putting them back. Wet cushions can create dye-transfer stains on your furniture.

Throws
· · · · · · · · · · · · · · · · ·

THROW RUGS AND BLANKETS ARE SUCH LOVELY ITEMS to snuggle up with on the couch while you watch a movie. Make sure to check the care instructions on the tag before cleaning your throw.

Most throws can be cleaned in a warm handwash or delicates cycle in the washing machine.

Some throws may be spot-clean only. Use a microfibre cloth dampened with warm water or upholstery spray to wipe any marks away. A vacuum and a good shake can help to prevent dust build-up.

Fireplace

. . . .

FIREPLACES CREATE SUCH A BEAUTIFUL ATMOSPHERE in your home, especially on cold winter nights.

Gas

Refer to your instruction manual before attempting to clean.

First, turn off the gas supply.

Use a soft brush to carefully remove any dirt and debris from the logs or rocks (if accessible). Use a vacuum to remove the dust and debris from the area.

With a microfibre cloth, use glass cleaner for any glass areas and stainless steel cleaner for the stainless steel surround.

Electric

Refer to your instruction manual before attempting to clean.

First, turn off the electricity supply.

Use a vacuum with a soft brush attachment to carefully remove any dust and debris from the unit and heating vents.

With a microfibre cloth, use glass cleaner for any glass areas or general-purpose spray for the housing.

Wood

Check that your fire is completely extinguished and completely cool.

Clear the ash from the fireplace as often as possible. You can use a heavy-duty workshop vacuum or ash vacuum, or use a dustpan to scoop the ash into a plastic bag. Do not use a household vacuum as the ash will damage the filters.

If your fireplace has a glass door, take a wet cloth and dip a corner into some of the removed ash. Use the ash and the cloth to rub over the glass door. This will remove any burn or smoke marks.

Wipe over your flue and any exposed housing with a damp cloth.

family bathroom/ ensuite

create a sparkling-clean area
to relax or get ready in

CLEANING THE FAMILY BATHROOM can be a bit like cleaning up after a huge storm has passed through.

Towels, clothing, toys and toothpaste all seem to end up in very interesting places. As a result, it can take a little while to get the bathroom back in top condition.

Clearing up the clutter is the best place to start. Take the washing to the laundry, hang any towels you plan to reuse, and put toys back in their tub or bag.

Follow the steps in our General Cleaning chapter to get the bones of your bathroom done. Then you can begin on the full bathroom clean to get your bathroom sparkling and ready for the next storm.

Drains

CLEANING YOUR DRAINS IS AN IMPORTANT STEP but it is likely to make a mess, so it's best to complete it before the rest of the bathroom.

To keep your drains flowing well, you need to ensure hair and other debris doesn't build up in the pipework. Bunnings sell small-drain cleaning tools that can be used without the need to hire a plumber. The easiest to use are the 'sink drain unblockers' – Bunnings sell the Kinetic brand. You simply slip the device down the plughole (if you have a pop-up push-plug, unscrew the top of it first) and, after a bit of a jiggle, drag it back up and dispose of the gunk. Repeat if necessary.

Surfaces

START BY SPRAYING ALL YOUR SURFACES – benchtops, sink, shower and screens, bath – with a general-purpose cleaner, or a solution of vinegar and water. Then, as you move from one area to the next, you are giving the surfaces time to have a little soak. This allows hardened spots to soften and become easier to clean.

Bathroom Sink
· · · · · · · · · · · · · · · ·

ALL SORTS OF YUCKY THINGS CAN BUILD UP in the bathroom sink. If you have small children, toothpaste is usually the main culprit.

If you have already sprayed your sink with a general-purpose cleaner, all that is needed is a wipe with a microfibre cloth. Around your plughole or overflow you may like to use a small brush, like a toothbrush or bottle brush, to get into the finer grooves. Now is a great time to use that brush around the tap base, too, to remove any built-up grime.

For stains and stubborn marks, you can use a paste made from bicarb and water. Pop a little of the paste onto a microfibre cloth and gently rub the mark to remove it.

Benchtops
· · · · · · · · · · · · · · · ·

SINCE YOU WILL HAVE ALREADY SPRAYED your benchtops, you can simply give them a wipe with a microfibre cloth to easily remove the stuck-on grime and marks. Wipe down your benchtop items before replacing them so that you are not placing dirty items onto a clean surface.

If you are time poor and don't have time for your benchtop to dry before placing your items back, use a dry, non-lint tea towel (e.g. White Magic brand) to dry the surface. Placing coloured items on the benchtop when wet may cause dye transfer.

Bath

CLEANING YOUR BATH IS BASICALLY THE SAME as cleaning a giant sink – use the same method as for the bathroom sink. If you have a defined water ring around your bath, you might like to use a cloth designed for bathrooms or tough marks. Bathroom cloths (such as the Nature Direct Shower Cloth) are generally a little tougher, and include tiny built-in scrubbers.

It is a good idea to give your bath a rinse after cleaning as some residue from cleaning products can remain. We don't want our little people sitting in that while having their bath.

Bath Toys

THERE ARE A FEW DIFFERENT TYPES OF BATH TOYS, but most can be cleaned in the same way.

Be wary of toys that are filled with air, squirt water or have holes that water can get into. These provide the perfect environment for mould to grow. You can seal these toys with a hot glue gun or silicone.

For other bath toys, you can clean them easily in a bucket or tub of vinegar and water – or, if you prefer, water and disinfectant. Let them soak for a few hours and then pop them out to dry.

A Strucket – a strainer-meets-bucket – is a great device for storing and cleaning bath toys. Fill the Strucket with vinegar and water and add the bath toys. Lift

the basket up and down a few times to agitate the water to make sure they get a good clean. Leave the toys to soak for a few hours.

Place the Strucket over the edge of a sink or drain so that the drain hole is exposed and open the plug. Lift the strainer and hook it onto the lip. Leave this to drain completely. You can leave the toys in the strainer, as the holes provide natural airflow and allow the toys to dry. Leave overnight or take the Strucket outside for some sunlight.

Shower

· · · · · · · · · · · · · · · ·

SHOWERS CAN BE MADE OF VARIOUS SURFACES. Some are fully tiled, while others have bases made from polymarble, acrylic and other materials. How you clean your shower will depend on what it is made of, but the methods are all similar.

Wall tiles

As you have already sprayed this surface, your next step will be determined by the condition of your grout. If your grout is in pretty good, clean condition, you can jump right into scrubbing each section with a grout brush. A grout brush is a really important tool for cleaning – it really does make the job a lot easier than using any other type of scrubbing brush.

If your grout is a bit mouldy or not looking its best, spray a grout-cleaning solution or some more general-purpose spray onto your tiles. Then, using the grout brush, scrub each section. You may also like to treat the area with some white vinegar to help prevent the mould from returning. Simply mix a 1:1 solution of water and vinegar and spray over the areas, and after a couple of minutes wipe or hose it off with your shower head. To avoid mould, ensure your bathroom is getting enough ventilation.

If you feel your grout is still not clean enough, have a look at our Cleaning Recipes section to see how to make a Polident solution. Many Mums Who Clean members have raved about the difference this has made to the appearance of their grout.

Once you are happy with your grout, use a microfibre cloth and give your tiles a good wipe all over.

If you have heavy scum build-up you can use a plastic or heavy-duty safety scraper to remove it before spraying and wiping with a general cleaning spray.

A Magic Eraser can also help to remove shower scum.

Shower grate

Shower grates can become mouldy and a bit gross looking. To clean them, you can give them a wipe with a microfibre cloth and a general-purpose spray.

If your shower grate is looking a bit rusted or corroded, you can use Bar

Keepers Friend Cleanser & Polish Powder to bring it back to life. Using a wet microfibre cloth and some of the powder, scrub the drain cover to remove the marks.

Shower base

Shower bases can be made of a few different materials.

Tiles

If your shower base is tiled, use the same steps as for wall tiles to clean the shower base tiles.

Polymarble or acrylic

Cleaning a polymarble or acrylic shower base is quite easy as it is a very durable surface. Using a general-purpose spray or liquid soap, give the base a wipe with a microfibre cloth.

Never use items like steel wool, scrubbing pads or products that are abrasive, as these will cause damage to the polymarble or acrylic, making it harder to clean in the future.

Commercial drain cleaners should also be avoided, as these can cause damage as well.

Shower screens

Cleaning shower screens is basically the same as cleaning windows – except for the soap scum.

You will have already sprayed this surface at the beginning of your cleaning. This will have helped the soap scum to loosen. Now give the screen another light spray and wipe with a microfibre or glass-cleaning cloth.

Mums Who Clean members have some of the most amazing advice for cleaning shower screens. Some of the most popular are:

Dishwashing liquid and vinegar

Fill a dishwand with a 1:1 solution of dishwashing liquid and white vinegar. Simply wet the wand and scrub the screen fully. Rinse with water or a wet cloth. You may also like to follow up with a dry glass-cleaning cloth for a sparkling finish.

Di-San Pre Wash Stain Remover

For heavy scum on shower screens, some members use Di-San Pre Wash Stain Remover, available only at Aldi. Spray all over the shower screen and scrub with a magic eraser or a cloth (depending on the amount of scum). Rinse the product off the screen thoroughly. Ensure you have a well-ventilated area and wear a mask, as this product can be a bit smelly.

Bar Keepers Friend Cleanser & Polish Powder (BKF)

BKF is probably one of the most talked-about products in the Mums Who Clean Facebook group. Every time a new member asks 'What can I use BKF for?', one of the first suggestions is always 'shower screens'.

Wet your shower screen and sprinkle BKF onto a wet microfibre cloth. Use appropriate force while scrubbing the soap scum from the screen. Rinse thoroughly with water. You will be left with a beautiful finish.

Shower curtains

Most fabric shower curtains can be washed on a delicate setting in the washing machine and then hung back up to dry.

If you have extra scum you want to remove, you can soak the curtain in Napisan before washing it in your machine.

If your curtain is not suitable for a washing machine you can use washing powder, warm water and a bristle brush.

Shower head

Built-up mineral deposits, dirt, dust and soap scum can clog up the shower head and affect the water flow.

You can clean your shower head by spraying it with a combination of vinegar and water. Leave this for a few minutes to soak in. Use a toothbrush to scrub the head gently to remove any build-up in the nozzles.

If you have a heavy build-up of limescale, you may need to soak your shower head. Soaking may cause damage to some units, so check your manufacturer's recommendations first.

If you have a detachable shower head, you can soak it in an appropriate tub, like an old ice cream container or a bucket. If your shower head is in a fixed position, fill a small plastic bag with your soaking solution and use an elastic band to attach it over the shower head.

Depending on the severity of the build-up, you can use a (1:1) vinegar and water solution or a descaling product such as Scalex Heavy Duty Home Descaler or CLR Calcium, Limescale & Rust Remover. These products have their own dilution instructions on the packaging.

Shower tracks and frames

You can easily clean your shower tracks and frames with a microfibre cloth and a general-purpose cleaner. For the tracks, you may find that some debris remains when using a cloth. If this occurs, use a small brush, such as a toothbrush, to remove it. This is especially helpful in the corners.

Shampoo and conditioner bottles

Before popping your shampoo and conditioner bottles back into the shower, give them a quick once-over with your microfibre cloth. Mould and grime can build up on the base where the bottles sit on the shelf or tiles.

Tapware
· · · · · · · · · · · · · · · · ·

TAPS AND SPOUTS CAN HAVE MANY DIFFERENT FINISHES, including chrome, brushed metal, brass and matt black. Most of these can be cleaned in the same way.

Most manufacturers recommend using warm water and a pH-neutral cleaner to wipe the surface with a microfibre cloth. Use a small, soft brush around the base of the fittings to remove any build-up. Dry the surface with a dry microfibre cloth when you have finished cleaning. Try to clean off any splashes of soap, toothpaste, shampoo or other products as they happen, as these can damage your tapware's finish.

Koh Universal Cleaner is an excellent product for tapware and is safe for most finishes. Simply spray a dry microfibre cloth with some Koh and wipe over and around the tap. As you are using a mostly dry cloth, there is no need to use a second cloth to dry it to achieve that sparkling clean look.

Avoid using steel wool or scrubbing pads as they may damage your finish, leaving it looking scratched and dirty.

Cabinets *and* Drawers

CLEAR A SPACE ON YOUR BENCHTOP or floor where you can place the items from your cabinets and drawers. Remove all the items from the cabinet, focusing on one cabinet or drawer at a time. Give the interior a vacuum to remove any dirt, hair and debris. Use a microfibre cloth with vinegar and water or a general-purpose cleaner to wipe the surfaces.

Mirrors

MIRRORS GET SPLASHED with all kinds of things, such as water, soap and toothpaste. These splashes look horrible and make the mirror hard to use.

As with most bathroom surfaces, you can use a general-purpose spray or a solution of vinegar and water. Spray the surface and give it a wipe with a glass-cleaning cloth.

Exhaust Fans

· · · · · · · · · · · · · · · ·

EXHAUST FANS ARE THE HARDEST-WORKING part of a bathroom. They gather all sorts of dust and grime while removing the steam and moisture from your room to prevent mould and mildew.

There are three main parts to your exhaust fan: the cover, fan blades and motor. Keeping your exhaust fan in top condition will prolong the life of the fan.

To deep-clean your fan, first you need to turn off the power to your bathroom at your fuse box. If you do not have good natural light, having a work light or torch available will be essential.

As exhaust fans are situated high in the ceiling or wall, make sure you have a stepladder or step stool that allows you to safely reach that height.

Rachael's *tip*

In between deep cleans you can use a cobweb broom to brush down any dust from the fan cover, then vacuum or mop up the debris when you do the rest of the bathroom.

Fan cover

Remove the fan cover. Your instruction manual will tell you how to do this. There are a few different ways that fan covers are attached. Some twist on and off, some have little clips and others are screwed on.

To clean the fan cover, soak it in some soapy water. This will help soften the build-up. Using a soft brush, like a bottle brush, scrub the cover to remove the dust and grime. You can also use a microfibre cloth to remove the build-up. The fan cover will need to be completely dry before reattaching.

Fan blades and motor

Again, check your instruction manual to see how your fan is attached, and check for any cleaning instructions for your particular brand.

We don't recommend removing your fan and motor from the ceiling.

This is an electrical device – only a professional should do this.

However, as you have turned the power off to your bathroom, you can give the fan blades and motor a clean while they're in place. Using a vacuum and a paintbrush, loosen and suck up all the dust and build-up that has gathered in your fan. Once you have done this, you may notice that your fan blades are still not as clean as they could be. Using a slightly damp microfibre cloth, give the blades a gentle wipe. Be very careful when doing this. As with light fittings, exhaust fans are electrical – we want to clean them, but we don't want to affect the electrical integrity of the fixture.

When you are happy with the clean, leave the cover off so that any areas you have wiped can dry thoroughly.

Once the fan and cover are completely dry, reattach the cover and turn your power back on.

Towels

THE BEST WAY TO KEEP YOUR TOWELS looking fluffy, fresh and new is to look after them from the moment you purchase them.

New towels

New towels come with a coating on them so they look inviting for customers. This coating, which may include fabric softener and silicone, reduces the absorbency of towels. If it is not removed, it can affect how your towels function.

Giving them a wash when you get them home is a great first move. Using warm water is recommended but if you only use cold water, that's okay: just add ½–1 cup of vinegar to the load, depending on your machine and load size. This will help remove the coating and get your new towels ready for use.

Regular washing

Towels are made to be absorbent and fluffy. Adding fabric softeners to the wash only reduces their absorbency.

A gentle laundry detergent is recommended, with an occasional ½ cup of vinegar added to help remove build up. Don't overload the machine – towels need extra room so the water can move around them.

Sometimes towels need a thorough cleaning, as normal cleaning is not always enough. Soaking them in a stain-removing product such as Napisan is a great option. A natural way to help keep towels clean is to pop them in the laundry tub or bath, add a cup of bicarb and fill with very hot water. You can do this with water from one or several kettles, then use the hottest water from your tap for the rest.

Leave the towels to soak for a few hours, until the water is cool. Let the water drain and wash your towels as you normally would.

Drying

For nice, soft, fluffy towels, remove them from the washing machine, give them a little shake and then pop them in the dryer. This opens up the fibres and gives the best result.

Karlie's *tip*

When washing towels, putting them through an extra rinse and spin cycle with ½ cup of vinegar in the fabric softener drawer can help towels retain their colour and fluffiness.

Karlie's *tip*

If you find your line-dried towels are stiff and scratchy, pop them in the dryer on the air-dry setting to soften for a few minutes or until the sensor turns it off.

If you don't have a dryer or don't want to use it, you can dry your towels on the clothesline. To help them retain their colours, keeping them in the shade is recommended.

Toiletries

. . . .

Hairbrushes

Hairbrushes can get a bit gross if not cared for. They are in contact with your hair and hair oils daily so need maintenance to ensure they are clean and ready for use.

A good routine to get into is to remove hair from your hairbrush every time you use it. You can do this easily with a pin tail comb (a comb with a long pointed 'tail'). Run the pointy end up and down the brush, lifting the hair so you can easily grab and remove it.

Cleaning your hairbrush with shampoo every so often will help to remove any oil or build-up. Take a bowl big enough to fit your brush's head in it, and fill with warm water and shampoo. Dip the head of your brush in this mixture for 1 minute. Using a small brush, like a straw brush or toothbrush, apply a small amount of shampoo and scrub the bristles and base of the hairbrush head. Rinse it off with clean water and leave it to dry, bristles facing down.

Do not submerge your brush in water for too long or leave bristles facing up to dry as this can cause liquid to build up and ruin your brush.

Toothbrushes

Toothbrushes are a breeding ground for germs. They are coated in all sorts of food waste and toothpaste, not to mention bacteria from your mouth.

Daily care

After brushing your teeth, rinse any remaining toothpaste or food waste from your brush. Stand your brush on its handle end, ensuring it has room to air-dry and is not touching other toothbrushes.

Dentists recommend replacing your toothbrush every 3–4 months, or when bristles are frayed or worn.

Sanitising

If you have been unwell, bacteria and viruses may survive on your toothbrush and be transmitted back to you or other members of your family.

There are a couple of ways to make sure this doesn't happen. Dipping the bristles in antibacterial mouthwash for 1 minute is a super easy way to sanitise your toothbrush. Discard the mouthwash after use.

If you don't have mouthwash, you can soak the bristles in straight vinegar overnight.

Make-up brushes

Make-up brushes harbour bacteria. This is the most important reason for cleaning them. Another good reason is that, over time, make-up deposits on the brushes can wear down the bristles, causing them to break.

Dirty make-up brushes and the bacteria in them can also contribute to skin break-outs and acne.

Washing brushes

How often you wash your brushes really depends on your personal preference and how often you use them.

There are a number of different products available for cleaning brushes. The easiest method is to use face cleanser or shampoo.

Run the bristles of your make-up brushes under warm water. Keep the bristles facing down – do not let the water run up the handle of the brush or it will loosen the glue holding your bristles in place.

Pour a little bit of cleanser or shampoo into a bowl. Lightly swirl the bristles around in the cleanser or shampoo. Then, using the palm of your hand or a make-up brush cleansing mat, swirl the brush around to loosen the make-up stuck to the bristles.

Rinse the brush under warm water and repeat the above process until the water runs clear.

If you have build-up that cannot be removed with this method, use a fine-tooth comb to help loosen it. Then repeat the process above until clean.

Depending on your cleaning method, the bristles can become a bit rough or coarse, making them feel unpleasant on your face. To rectify this, add a little conditioner to your brushes after every second or third clean. Make sure you rinse thoroughly.

Sometimes doing all this cleaning can warp the shape of your brush a little. You can use the palm of your hand and fingers to reshape the brush back into the correct form before drying.

Drying brushes

There are some specially designed holders on the market that make drying your brushes easier. However, if you don't have one of these, you can easily dry your brushes using a towel.

Roll the end of a towel over two or three times. Lay your bushes on the towel, with the handles propped up on the rolled end so that the water doesn't trickle back towards the brush glue. Leave the brushes to dry overnight.

Once dry, gently run the bristles over your hand to make sure they feel nice and soft before use.

toilet
room

how to keep the throne
clean and the area fresh

THE TOILET ROOM (or the area around the toilet, if yours is in the main bathroom) can get dusty and smelly quite easily.

Dust in the toilet room or around the toilet is increased by the fibres from toilet paper. Wiping the surfaces, including the toilet exterior, with a dust cloth first will make cleaning them a lot simpler.

Then use a cloth sprayed with general-purpose cleaner to clean the exterior of the toilet, including the outer section of the rim.

Toilet Seat

TAKE THE TOILET SEAT OFF! Taking the toilet seat off regularly for a clean is a must. Each seat will be slightly different but usually very easy to remove. Unclip the seat, then use a general-purpose spray and a cloth to clean the gunk under the clips (and the clips themselves). Wipe over the whole toilet seat and then pop the seat back on.

Toilet Bowl

TO KEEP YOUR TOILET FRESH AND CLEAN, it's easiest to use a toilet brush with your preferred cleaner. You may like to use commercial toilet cleaner or even a general-purpose cleaner. The method is similar for each type of cleaner: squirt, spray or sprinkle the cleaner into the toilet and use your toilet brush to scrub the product in and around the bowl. Once cleaned, flush the toilet with the brush in the stream of the fresh water. Place the toilet brush handle under the toilet seat, with the brush suspended over the bowl, so it can dry.

For a more natural clean you can use bicarb and vinegar. Sprinkle bicarb around the bowl. Pour vinegar over the bicarb to create a fizzing reaction. Give a quick scrub with your toilet brush and flush once done.

Toilet bombs

Toilet bombs are an easy and effective way to clean your toilet bowl. You will find how to make these in our Cleaning Recipes chapter.

Pop 1 or 2 toilet bombs into your toilet bowl. Leave for a few hours to fizz and clean your bowl. Flush your toilet as usual and your toilet bowl will be clean.

Limescale

Brown marks inside your toilet bowl? These stubborn scale marks are often unsightly and very difficult – or seemingly impossible – to remove with just a toilet brush and toilet cleaner.

To remove these marks, all you need is Scalex Heavy Duty Home Descaler. Tip ⅓ cup into the toilet bowl and wait as long as possible before scrubbing with your toilet brush – overnight is best. If the scale is severe, you may need to do this twice.

Another option is to use citric acid. Use the same method as for Scalex, above.

Toilet brush

Clean your toilet brush by sitting the brush part in a bucket of water mixed with white vinegar or disinfectant for a few hours. Allow to dry in the sun if possible.

Tiles

TO CLEAN SMELLY TILES, you might need to do more than just mop. Once the room is cleaned, spread shaving foam over the floor tiles and around the base of the toilet where it meets the floor. Leave the shaving foam on the floor for 30 minutes, then mop with hot water to remove the residue. The shaving foam will remove any urine smells that might be lingering.

Louvre Windows

A LOT OF TOILET ROOMS HAVE LOUVRE WINDOWS, especially in older homes. They get very dirty, very fast. To clean your louvre window, carefully remove each pane of glass – usually you tug upwards, following the angle of the louvre. Fill your laundry tub or trough with hot water and dishwashing liquid. Place the louvre panes into the water one by one and wash thoroughly with a cloth. Lay them on a dry towel to dry completely before placing them back into the slots.

If your louvre panes cannot be removed, use a damp cloth between a pair of tongs or a louvre cleaning brush to wipe the glass.

laundry

get your washing done quickly,

easily and efficiently

THE LAUNDRY IS OFTEN FORGOTTEN ABOUT in household cleaning, but it is important to address it. Dirty clothes, shoes and kids' messes all get stored here, waiting to be cleaned. A dryer can also create quite a lot of dust as lint floats around.

The best way to start cleaning your laundry is to first try to do as much of your clothes washing as possible in the days leading up to your laundry clean. This gets it out of your way, and also helps with your overall clean-up.

Cabinets *and* Drawers

· · · · · · · · · · · · · · · · ·

REMOVE THE ITEMS FROM THE CABINET (including your broom closet and linen closet). Use a vacuum with a brush attachment to remove any dust and debris. Wipe down the cabinets and drawers, inside and out, using a general-purpose spray or a solution of water and vinegar. You can also wipe the benchtops now too.

Laundry Tub/Trough

· · · · · · · · · · · · · · · · · ·

YOU CAN CLEAN YOUR LAUNDRY TUB OR TROUGH, and its splashback, in a similar way to your kitchen sink and splashback – see the Kitchen chapter for details.

Wipe over your splashback with a general-purpose cleaner and a microfibre cloth.

Paint in the trough

If your tub/trough is stainless steel and has become covered in paint from DIY projects, you can clean it using dishwasher tablets.

Place the plug in your tub/trough and line the walls and base with aluminium foil. Fill the tub with hot water so it covers the paint-affected areas, and place 3 or 4 dishwasher tablets in the water (depending on the size of your tub). Let the tub soak for a few hours. When you come back, discard the foil and give the tub a light scrub before draining the water.

Washing Machine

THE WASHING MACHINE IS ALSO OFTEN FORGOTTEN in home cleaning. A lot of people assume that because it is used for washing, it is already clean. However, like most appliances, it needs to be cleaned regularly to ensure it can do its job properly.

Laundry detergents, stain removers, fabric softeners and residue from dirty clothing can remain in the machine after the wash is done. Most instruction manuals recommend cleaning your machine monthly or after a certain number of loads. There are several ways to do this.

To help keep your machine clean, always remove the clothing as soon as possible after the cycle is finished. Leaving the machine door or lid open after each wash is also helpful as it allows the drum to dry out. This is especially important if you have a front-loading machine – leaving the door open helps to prevent mould building up in the seal around the door.

If you wash especially dirty clothing, such as tradie clothing, debris can get left in your machine. Once the machine is dry, use your vacuum to suck this stuff up.

Wipe down the outside of your machine using a general-purpose cleaner.

Seal

If you have a front-loading machine, wipe the rubber seal around the door. You can do this with a damp cloth sprayed with vinegar or a suitable cleaning product, such as a general-purpose cleaner. Then use a dry cloth to dry the seal.

Detergent drawer

Take out the detergent drawer, scrub any residue off and leave this to dry.

If you have hard-to-remove build-up, you can soak the detergent drawer in warm water to soften it.

Once this is dry, pop it back into your machine so that it is ready to go.

Drum

Many machines have a drum-clean cycle, which is a very hot wash cycle that you run without any clothes in the machine. If your machine has this feature, follow the advice in the manual to ensure you avoid damaging your machine. Don't add any cleaning products to the machine in a drum-clean cycle unless the manual specifically advises you to do so.

If you generally use only cold water to wash your clothing, turn on the hot tap for this clean. Using hot water is very important. Some machines heat the water themselves – if your machine does this, you will not need to turn on the hot tap.

If your machine does not have a drum-clean cycle, you can manually run a hot cycle yourself.

There are a number of different products you can use to keep smells at bay and remove build-up from your machine. Most of these are available at your local supermarket. Epsom salts is often suggested for this task, but you need to be careful – salt can promote rust, which is not something you want in your washing machine.

Vinegar and bicarb

There is no exact recipe for cleaning your machine with vinegar and bicarb. It's really a matter of personal preference. However, approximately 1 tablespoon of bicarb and 1/2–1 cup of vinegar are good amounts.

Add the bicarb to the detergent drawer, then pour the vinegar into the drum. Run your machine on its hottest cycle.

If you haven't cleaned your machine regularly, you may notice a lot of suds. This is normal and will reduce each time you clean your machine as the build-up will reduce. It is also a good idea to run a hot rinse cycle after this to rinse the drum – you don't want those extra suds in with your next normal wash.

Leave the door or lid open so that your machine dries.

Filter

You will need to read the machine's manual for the best advice on finding and opening the filter. Locate your machine's filter, then remove and clean as per manufacturer's instructions.

Dryer

· · · · · · · · · · · · · · · · ·

CLEANING YOUR DRYER IS SO IMPORTANT to maintain fire safety. How you clean your dryer will depend on the type of dryer you have. However, you can begin the clean for most machines in the same way.

First, using a general-purpose cleaner, wipe down the outside of your machine.

Lint filter

The next step is to clean out your lint filter. Make sure the machine is off, then remove the lint filter and discard the lint. Give the filter a thorough wipe and leave to dry.

Now grab your vacuum and clean the dryer's drum and the surrounds of the lint filter. This is an easy way to remove any lint that didn't make it into the filter.

If the area around your filter is still not clean enough, use a microfibre cloth or a bottle brush to remove the remaining lint.

Using the cloth, wipe down the door, seal and drum.

It is really important to remove as much lint from your dryer as possible on a regular basis. A build-up of lint, even a little bit, can cause a fire.

Vented dryer

If you have a vented dryer, the steps above for cleaning the lint filter are all you will need to do.

Condenser and heat pump dryer

If you have a condenser dryer, you have a few extra cleaning steps.

First, remove the condensation tray and give this a rinse. If it has a smell or isn't looking clean, you can add some vinegar and bicarb to the tray. Add water and leave it to sit for a few minutes, then rinse thoroughly. Leave this to dry.

You will also need to clean the condenser by removing this from the machine and cleaning according to the manufacturer's instructions. Most recommend you rinse the condenser with a tap or pressure washer until it runs clear. The fins can be quite sharp, so be careful not to cut yourself. Leave to dry and then pop back in the machine.

You will also need to wipe the heat sensors to remove any build-up. You can do this with a damp cloth, with a little vinegar added if you prefer.

master
bedroom

you'll sleep easy once you've

mastered this chapter

THE MASTER BEDROOM IS OFTEN one of the most overlooked areas of a home when it comes to cleaning. Life is busy, and we all tend to clean the areas we see during the day. Bedrooms can become dumping grounds for items that don't have a home or that we don't have time to put away properly.

Once you have finished the tasks from the General Cleaning chapter, you can start on a more thorough clean.

Bedside Tables

DUST OFF THE BEDSIDE TABLES with a dry microfibre cloth. Use a general-purpose cleaner to quickly wipe over the top and sides, if required. Empty the drawers and vacuum the interior. Clear out any rubbish that has accumulated and get things back in order.

Karlie's *tip*

Small baskets on bedside tables and in bedside drawers help to keep the space defined and make the area easier to clean.

Ornaments *and* Decorative Items

WIPE OVER ORNAMENTS, DECORATIVE ITEMS, photo frames and lamp bases with a microfibre cloth. A lint roller is a quick, easy and effective way to remove dust from lampshades.

Intricate items can be dusted thoroughly with a small dusting brush or paintbrush.

Tallboys *and* Storage

CLEAN TALLBOYS, CHESTS OF DRAWERS and storage furniture by emptying them out and vacuuming. Wipe over the interior if required. Return your items, then wipe everything down with a general-purpose spray and a microfibre cloth.

If you have a TV in your bedroom, this is the perfect time to clean that too. You can do this by following the tips in the Lounge Room chapter.

If you have under-bed storage, pull that out and give it a vacuum.

Wardrobes

USE A VACUUM with a crevice tool (the long, thin attachment) to clean out the debris left by shoes, bags and accessories. Wipe all surfaces down with a microfibre cloth and general-purpose spray to remove any settled dust.

Go through your clothing and make sure everything is sorted and in the correct place. A general tidying of the area just makes everything feel ordered and calm.

Bedhead

HOW YOU CLEAN YOUR BEDHEAD will depend on what type of bedhead you have.

A sticky lint roller is an excellent tool for cleaning a fabric bedhead.

Roll the lint roller over the surfaces of the bedhead to remove dust, pet hair and other debris. You can also use a vacuum with an upholstery attachment to do this.

Use an upholstery cleaner to spray any marks on the fabric and use a microfibre cloth to work the product in. Dry the area well with a white towel to avoid dye transfer and water marks.

Wooden and metal bedheads can be wiped down with a microfibre cloth dampened with a general-purpose cleaner.

Bed Linen and Bedding
. . . .

HOW OFTEN YOU CHANGE YOUR BED LINEN and bedding is a personal decision. Getting into a good routine that suits your lifestyle will make things easier and ensure that your bedding lasts as long as possible.

General washing

How you wash your bed linen – sheets, pillowcases, doona covers and throws – will depend on the material each item is made from. Most bed linen can be put into your washing machine on the cycle you use for your clothing; for bulkier items, you can use your machine's bedding cycle if it has one. Make sure to check the item's care label before deciding how to wash it.

There are a lot of products on the market that improve your laundry detergent or contain a boosting agent. These products can help with keeping colours bright and whites white. Power of 4 Laundry Powder, Omo Touch of Comfort powder, and even Napisan can help. Each product is a little different so the best one will depend on the type of fabric you're washing.

Soaking bed linen can also help to keep it looking good. A home remedy you can use for white bed linen is a mix of hot water, vinegar, bicarb and any laundry detergent. Sunshine is a very effective, natural and free way to bleach your bed linen white.

A Strucket can be an effective tool for soaking bed linen. The strainer that moves up and down creates good agitation to help the solution move through the fabric. The strainer can also be lifted up and attached to the side of the bucket to allow the water to drain, alleviating you of the need to wring the linen out. The plug at the bottom allows the water to drain without you needing to lift a heavy bucket of water.

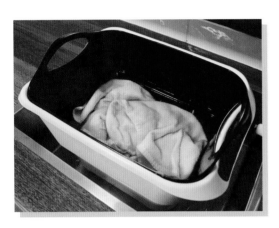 

Many items of bed linen can be dried in the dryer. Adding a dryer ball can be helpful to prevent sheets and doona covers from getting tangled, and can reduce drying time as they increase airflow through the fabric.

Mattress and pillow protectors

Mattress and pillow protectors can save a lot of time on cleaning. They protect the items that are hardest to clean and are just as easy to remove and to wash as your other bed linen. These are especially helpful in keeping spills off mattresses and pillows, and at times like toilet-training or during illness.

Doonas and blankets

Your doonas and blankets also need to be washed. Most doonas and many blankets can be washed in your washing machine. It may be helpful to add some clean tennis balls to help doonas move around and clean well in the wash. Make sure you check your care tags before choosing to wash this way.

It is especially important to follow care instructions if your doona is made with wool or filled with feathers. Heat can cause wool to shrink, so washing with cool water and drying inside on a clothes airer is a great way to go. Feathers may move around inside the doona and clump, and it can be very difficult to correct this. Handwashing may be best.

Once your washing cycle is complete, you can either use your dryer or hang your item to dry. If you decide to use your dryer, make sure you pop in a couple of dryer balls to keep things moving with ease.

If you are using your washing machine and/or dryer to clean large items it is important to ensure your machine's weight capacity is sufficient. Each machine will have a different weight rating and it is important to know yours and how it works. Most domestic washing machines have a weight rating of between 7 and 16 kilograms. (This is the weight of the washing when dry.) Not all cycles will hold the full capacity so read your manual to ensure you are using the best wash cycle for your load. Many dryers have a significantly lower weight rating but the weight is still measured when the load is dry, not wet.

If your machine cannot handle the weight, many laundromats offer a doona-cleaning service, or you can simply use their larger capacity machines for a fee.

Pillows

Most pillows can be washed using the same methods as for your doona or blankets. Pillows are, however, best dried on a flat surface in sunlight. Sunlight helps to whiten the pillow (as most are white) but also to sanitise the fabric and filling. Some pillows may also be dried in the dryer. Add some dryer balls to prevent the filling clumping inside the pillow.

Before deciding on your drying method, check the care instructions on the tag.

kids' bedrooms

create a clean space the kids
will actually want to go to bed in

CLEANING A CHILD'S BEDROOM is quite similar to cleaning a master bedroom. Kids' rooms can get a bit grubby if you don't keep on top of the tidying and cleaning, so if this is your first time doing the room thoroughly, allow plenty of time. After the big clean, you will only need to maintain it, so less time will be needed.

It is a good idea to begin with a quick tidy of the room, searching in all the places that kids tend to hide or drop things. Under the bed, under pillows, under furniture, in the back of the wardrobe and inside drawers are all places to check. Grab the kids' 'collections' and pop them away – place them in a tub to deal with later.

Furniture

· · · · · · · · · · · · · · · · · · ·

FOR ANY DRAWERS AND SHELVES, remove all the items and use a dusting cloth to dust down the furniture. Wipe over the outer surfaces with a general-purpose cleaner and a microfibre cloth.

Having a vacuum handy is a good idea too, as kids seem to bring sand, dirt, leaves, crumbs and a variety of other crud into their rooms, which accumulates on shelves and in drawers.

Bed Linen *and* Bedding

· · · · · · · · · · · · · · · · ·

KIDS' BED LINEN CAN BE CLEANED using the tips in the Master Bedroom chapter.

If your child is toilet-training, it can be helpful to double-layer their sheets. To do this, place a waterproof mattress protector on top of the mattress, then pop on a sheet as usual. On top of this, place another waterproof mattress

protector and sheet. If your child has an accident in the middle of the night, you only need to remove the top layer of bedding – no need to remake the bed. It makes things much easier.

If you don't have two mattress protectors, puppy-training pads are a great alternative. You can

place these under the sheet to protect the mattress or the second sheet. If there is an accident, you can just pop the sheet in the washing machine and the puppy-training pad in the bin.

How to Get Kids Involved in Cleaning

· · · · · · · · · · · · · · · · ·

MOST PEOPLE DON'T REALLY WANT TO CLEAN, especially kids. But teaching your kids this valuable life lesson will make things easier for everyone in the long term. Getting the kids to help doesn't need to be stressful for anyone, but it's important to set guidelines and to understand that they probably won't do the job perfectly.

Little kids generally love to vacuum or use a spray bottle. It's a great idea to fill a spray bottle with water and let your kids use that with a cloth to clean the kitchen cabinets or skirting boards. This doubles as a distraction, so you can get some of your daily tasks crossed off your list.

Ask them to do small tasks that directly benefit them – for example, packing away the toys in their toy room or bedroom will give them a nice space to play in the next day. Once they master this step you could put them in charge of vacuuming, etc. Start small and work up as your child learns and gains experience.

Older children just beginning to get involved in household chores might find a reward system beneficial. Rewards can be screen time, pocket money or special outings with Mum or Dad. Everyone has their own 'currency', so find what suits you and your child best.

Families with teenagers might like to use a family chore chart. Clearly defining the tasks each family member is responsible for takes nagging out of the equation. If everyone can see what they need to do, things should run a lot smoother.

It can be a struggle to see a cleaning task done to a much lower standard than you're used to, but the kids will refine their methods over time.

spare **bedroom**

put your guests at ease

with these quick cleaning tips

A SPARE BEDROOM CAN SERVE MANY FUNCTIONS – a place for guests to sleep, a storage area, a study, or a combination of these.

How you clean this room will depend on how you use it, but for the most part it will be similar to cleaning a master bedroom.

If you use your guest bedroom as a bit of a dumping ground for items without a home, remove these from your cleaning area by placing them in a tub or in the wardrobe to sort out later.

If you use the room as a study, you can move on to the Office/Study chapter.

Furniture

· · · · · · · · · · · · · · · · · ·

WIPE DOWN ALL SURFACES AND FURNITURE, as you would for the master bedroom and kids' bedrooms.

Bed Linen *and* Bedding

· · · · · · · · · · · · · · · · · ·

IN A GUEST BEDROOM, you generally don't need to change the bed linen as often as you do in a bedroom in constant use. Changing it before a guest arrives or after a guest leaves is sufficient. If you find the bedding is looking dusty but it doesn't need to be washed, you can shake it outside and air it on the clothesline.

When you are ready to wash the bed linen, you can wash it as described in the Master Bedroom chapter.

office/
study

declutter your workspace and
make getting organised easy

WHETHER YOU WORK FROM HOME or have a study for general tasks, it is often the room in the house where random items pile up. Items that don't have a home get dumped for later sorting and it can often take quite a while before you get to them.

To start, pack these items into a tub to deal with once your cleaning is complete.

Desk

• • • • • • • • • • • • • • • • • •

ONCE YOU HAVE CLEANED ALL the items on the desk (computer, printer, etc.), wipe down your desktop with a microfibre cloth and a general-purpose cleaner, or a solution of water and vinegar. Cleaning the work surface after you have finished cleaning all the other items will save you from doing the job twice.

Drawers

Desk drawers can get out of control very easily – a lot of items just get shoved in them. Before attempting to clean the drawers, empty them completely.

Give the interior of the drawers a thorough vacuuming and wipe down with a microfibre cloth and general-purpose spray.

Place your items back into the correct drawers, removing any items that don't belong.

Computer/Laptop

. . . .

COMPUTERS AND LAPTOPS GATHER a lot of dust. It is important to keep them clean, as dust, crumbs and stickiness can affect how they function.

Screen

Cleaning a computer monitor or laptop screen is very similar to cleaning a flat screen TV. Screens are prone to scratching and damage so be very careful when cleaning them.

Dust the screen and outer edges first. A screen-cleaning cloth, microfibre cloth or wool duster will work well. If you find marks difficult to remove, use a microfibre cloth with a little water. Make sure that the cloth is just barely damp – not wet. Then dry with a clean, dry microfibre cloth. Some brands may differ in their instructions so check the manual prior to cleaning.

Do not use window cleaner, soap or any chemicals as these can damage the screen's non-reflective coating.

Keyboard

All sorts of things can get stuck between the keys of a keyboard. Dust, dirt, hair and crumbs all gather in there, which can prevent the keys from functioning properly.

First, ensure your keyboard is disconnected from any power and remove any batteries. If you are using a laptop, switch the laptop off.

Use a can of compressed air to blow into the keyboard around the keys to dislodge anything stuck in there. If you prefer, you can use a vacuum (but be careful not to lose any keys!). There is a tool called a Dust Daddy that may fit your vacuum – it can make cleaning small areas like this easier. You can also use a hair dryer, on its cool setting, to blow debris out of the keyboard. The smaller nozzle will give the best results.

Using a clean microfibre cloth with a solution of vinegar and water, or with isopropyl alcohol, wipe the keyboard until it is clean. You can use a cotton bud or a small bottle brush to clean between the keys. Ensure that no liquid gets to the interior.

Mouse or trackpad

The mouse can get a little sticky. Whether it's from kids' hands, food crumbs or dust, this stickiness can have an impact on how your mouse works.

Start by unplugging the mouse from your computer and turning it off or removing the batteries. If you're cleaning your laptop trackpad, ensure the laptop is turned off.

Using a microfibre cloth and water, wipe the mouse or trackpad. Make sure that the cloth is not wet but only slightly damp. Allow the mouse or trackpad to dry completely before using.

If you use a mousepad, make sure that you give it a good clean by wiping it over with a clean cloth. You can use water and, if needed, you can add a little dishwashing soap. Avoid wetting any silicone backing – this may affect its non-slip performance. Let your mousepad completely air-dry before use.

Printer

· · · · · · · · · · · · · · · · ·

CLEANING A PRINTER IS QUITE EASY but make sure you follow any cleaning instructions and safety recommendations in the printer's manual.

Unplug the printer. Use a dusting cloth to dust down its outer surface and, if needed, use a microfibre cloth dampened with a general-purpose spray to clean any spills or grimy buttons.

Note

Do not pull your printer apart or try to clean the internal components unless you have experience or technical knowledge.

Filing *and* Paperwork

· · · · · · · · · · · · · · · · ·

PAPERWORK IS ONE OF THOSE THINGS that everyone seems to have too much of. No one likes sorting it. Once it piles up, it takes a long time to organise.

If you can, going paperless is a very neat and easy way to avoid this clutter. If you can't, create a good filing system so that putting the paperwork away is much easier.

For cleaning purposes, pop your paperwork into a to-do tray and focus on it at a later time.

To clean a filing cabinet or drawer, remove the hanging files and use your vacuum to remove any dust and debris. If required, you can then wipe it out with a microfibre cloth and general-purpose spray. Replace the files. In a standalone filing cabinet, it is important to empty only one drawer at a time to prevent the cabinet from overbalancing.

Use a similar method for the interior of any filing tubs, and dust the exterior.

Open Shelving

· · · · · · · · · · · · · · · · ·

OPEN SHELVING IS WHERE DUST LOVES TO LIVE, but it is also a great storage option for many people as it's so quick to access.

Remove the items and give the shelves a wipe down with a microfibre cloth and general-purpose spray.

Cleaning Kit

· · · · · · · · · · · · · · · · ·

KEEPING A SMALL KIT IN YOUR OFFICE so you can clean desk items more regularly is a great idea. Include a screen-cleaning cloth and a small microfibre cloth to take care of little smudges or spots of grime as you work. You might want to wipe your calculator, stapler or pen – having the tools on hand ensures the job isn't forgotten in your big clean.

toy room/ **games room**

free up space for activities
with these handy tips

TOY ROOMS AND GAMES ROOMS can become messy very quickly, especially when you have little kids who like to tip things out but haven't yet mastered the art of packing up. Toy rooms really benefit from organisation. Make sure every item has a specific home.

To begin your clean, tidy up all the toys and put them where they belong. Once the toys are packed up there is not a lot left to do – you will have taken care of most of it in the General Cleaning chapter.

However, you might come across some really tricky-to-clean areas in the toy room. Here's how to deal with them.

Slime on Carpet *or* Fabric
• • • • • • • • • • • • • • • •

TIP WHITE VINEGAR OVER THE HARDENED SLIME. Let it soak in to soften the slime, then gently remove as much as you can with a blunt scraping tool. Use an old towel to soak up as much vinegar as possible.

Use a wet vacuum (e.g. a Bissell SpotClean machine) if you have one. If you are working with hand tools only, keep scraping gently and dabbing the area with a clean towel to remove all the slime. You may then have a stain to remove from your carpet. See the Carpeted Floors section in the General Cleaning chapter for tips on stain removal.

If your fabric is delicate use caution.

Play Mats
• • • • • • • • • • • • • • • • •

A SIMPLE SOLUTION OF VINEGAR AND WATER is sufficient for play mats – just spray and wipe over.

If you need something stronger to remove stubborn marks, non-toxic cleaners include Koh Universal Cleaner

Karlie's *tip*

You can also use the vinegar and water solution in your spray mop and mop the surface of the mat.

and TRUEECO Everyday Cleaner. Simply spray the product and wipe it over. Use only a soft cloth to avoid scratching or compromising the mat's surface.

Fabric Boxes

· · · · · · · · · · · · · · · · ·

CUBE UNITS ARE REALLY POPULAR for toy room storage. If you have fabric boxes in your cube unit then you'll know that they can get grubby, quickly.

To clean the fabric boxes, you need to be careful not to get them too wet. The interior is often made of cardboard so getting them wet will ruin the structural integrity of the boxes. Spray a cloth with upholstery cleaner and spot-clean or wipe over the fabric surface.

Toys

· · · · · · · · · · · · · · · · ·

CLEANING TOYS IS IMPORTANT TO STOP the spread of germs after illness, and to ensure grime doesn't build up and prevent toys from working properly. Each type of toy needs different care.

You might like to use eco-friendly or natural products for peace of mind.

Be sure to check care labels and their instructions for cleaning your toys.

If you're cleaning up after an infection has been through your home, you might like to clean or spray toys with a sanitiser such as Nature Direct EnviroMist.

Hard plastic toys with no electrical components

These types of toys can be cleaned a number of ways. You can place the toys into a mesh laundry bag and put them into a bath or sink of hot soapy water. Swish the bag around before hanging the whole thing on the clothesline to dry. You can also tip the toys onto a towel to dry.

For larger toys, skip the mesh bag and pop the toys straight into a sink or bath filled with hot soapy water.

Some hard toys are suitable for the dishwasher too! Try to choose toys that won't collect dirty water in lips or crevices.

Rachael's *tip*
Use a Strucket to clean the smaller toys – it will speed up the process.

Plastic toys with electrical components

You need to ensure you don't get any of the electrical components wet. For these types of toys it's best to just wipe over with a damp cloth and a general-purpose cleaner.

Soft toys

Most of the time, soft toys can be spot-cleaned with a damp cloth. If you have soft toys that need further cleaning, the washing machine is a great option (unless the toy has electrical components). Just pop the toys into a mesh laundry bag, put the bag in the washing machine and run a delicates cycle. Once the cycle is finished, lay the toys flat on a clothes airer to dry fully before using them again. Drying in the sunshine is an excellent way to naturally sanitise the fibres.

If your toys are quite delicate or very special, then handwashing them in the laundry tub may be a safer option. Dry them on a flat surface such as a clothes airer.

Wooden toys

A wipe-over with a damp cloth is all that's needed. If wooden toys get too wet, they may become water damaged and swell, so it's best to avoid submerging them in water.

Craft Mess

IF YOUR KIDS GET INTO THE STATIONERY supplies, these tips will help you clean up quick smart!

Crayon on walls/furniture

Mayonnaise rubbed over the crayon does a superb job of removing the marks. Wipe the mayonnaise off with a general-purpose spray and a cloth.

If the mark is on a gloss finish, you might prefer to use only a general-purpose spray. Baby wipes are a great back-up if your marks are stubborn.

Pen or texta on walls/furniture

Simply spraying the area with hairspray and rubbing with a cloth will remove the ink from almost all surfaces. Hand sanitiser is also great but it should not be used on varnished surfaces.

Glitter

A dropped tub of glitter is possibly a parent's worst nightmare – you'll be finding glitter in every crevice for the next decade! A strip of packing tape can help to pick up the glitter really well. You can easily press the tape into crevices without disturbing the glitter and spreading it even further.

Rachael's *tip*
If the glitter is on a flat surface, a sticky lint roller will pick it up quickly.

Paint

On hard surfaces, wipe the paint as soon as possible. Most kids' paints should wipe off with just water and a soft cloth.

On clothing or fabric, a wash cycle in the washing machine should also be enough. Use a cycle that is about an hour long rather than a quick cycle. If the stain remains, use laundry liquid and a washboard or nailbrush to rid the item of the stain.

Stickers

Kids are amazingly creative! Finding a pad of stickers may seem like a dream come true to them. If your darlings put stickers everywhere, don't panic – they can be easy to remove!

First, try peeling the sticker off with your fingers. Get off as much as you can this way. If you're left with a sticky residue or the backing paper, put some eucalyptus oil on a cloth and dab the spot. Leave it for 1 minute, then wipe it away. Some stickers may need a few applications before they lift off.

Alternatively you can use a product like De-Solv-it Sticky Spot and Stain Remover or Orange Power Sticky Spot & Goo.

Karlie's *tip*
If the stickers are still not budging, use a hair dryer on a warm setting to loosen the adhesive. The sticker will then come away more easily.

porch

don't forget to give a little

attention to the front door

A PORCH IS OFTEN THE FIRST PART of your home that you or your guests see. It feels so welcoming to step into a clean porch or entrance area. Being outside, though, the area can get dirty quite fast. Keeping on top of the cleaning is a big help so that it doesn't become a huge job.

Use a cobweb broom to remove all the cobwebs around the door, windows and ceiling (if the area is covered). The cobweb broom is also an excellent heavy-duty duster so wipe away any dust as you go, including on bricks, weatherboards and concrete.

You may like to clean any windows now, or you may prefer to do all the windows in your home at the same time. For window-cleaning advice, see the Windows section in the General Cleaning chapter.

Screen Door
. . . .

YOU MAY BE ABLE TO PRESSURE-WASH your screen door without removing it – just make sure your other doors are watertight or you'll have a big mess to clean inside! If your other doors and windows aren't watertight, you can take your screen door off and pressure-wash outside. If you don't have a pressure washer, you can use a soft broom and a bucket of soapy water to scrub the door down.

Using water and vinegar to wash down the door is a great solution if you don't have space to remove the door and wash it down outside. Combine 1/3 cup vinegar and 4 cups of water in a bucket or tub. Grab a cloth and soak it in the solution, wring it out and wipe over all the parts of your screen door. You may need to change your cloth several times if you live in a particularly dusty area or near construction works.

Door *and* Window Frames

· · · · · · · · · · · · · · · ·

ONCE THE SCREEN DOOR IS DONE, wipe over the front door. A general-purpose cleaner and a cloth does the trick. Don't forget the door handle and the threshold.

Now use a cloth and general-purpose spray to wipe all the window frames. If you have handrails or balustrade rails, clean these using the same method. (If you used the water-and-vinegar method for the screen door, you can use that solution on your front door and windows too.)

Doormat

· · · · · · · · · · · · · · · · · · ·

MOST OF THE TIME, A GOOD SHAKE is sufficient to remove the stuck-in debris. Then just sweep the floor and discard the debris.

If you find your doormat needs a deeper clean, you can use a pressure washer to blast it. Hang the mat to dry, thoroughly, before replacing.

garage
and
driveway

pull up to a tidy space

with these tips

GARAGES GET DUSTY AND DIRTY very quickly. They have lots of different uses – storage, parking vehicles, woodwork, craft projects, hanging washing and more. Your garage may be the entrance to your home that you use most often.

Cobwebs can develop quickly in forgotten areas like the garage, so start by using a cobweb broom to remove all the cobwebs from the cornices, shelves and benchtops.

A blower is an ideal tool for cleaning the garage and driveway. Tidy up anything that isn't in its place and then use the blower to move dust, dirt and debris out the front or into a corner where you can more easily sweep or vacuum it up. Continue along the driveway to deal with leaf litter and dirt.

If you don't have a blower, use a heavy-duty duster or dusting cloth to wipe over anything that is stored in the garage.

Use a cloth and a general-purpose spray to wipe over benchtops, work spaces, furniture, shelves, tubs and so on.

Vacuum or sweep up all the debris on the floor.

For the exterior of the garage door, you can use a soft broom and soapy water to clean the surface if necessary. If it's just dusty, the cobweb broom may be the best tool to use. (Some garage door manufacturers have specific advice, so always check first.)

Spills *and* Messes

SPILLS AND MESSES ARE COMMON occurrences in a regularly used garage and on the driveway. Cars leak, containers are dropped and feet in dirty shoes walk all over these areas. Keeping on top of these messes will help to keep your garage and driveway looking clean and tidy.

Oil spills

Ensure you have good ventilation and there are no naked flames near the spill before beginning.

If you catch the spill quickly, throw some clay kitty litter (not the clumping kind) onto the oil right away and let the spill soak into the granules. Leave for 20 minutes or more depending on the size of the spill. Wearing gloves and a mask, scoop up the soaked litter and place it into a garbage bag. (Coolant spills can also be cleaned in this way.) Ensure you dispose of the waste appropriately.

If you don't have kitty litter available, you can use flour (plain or cornflour) or even sawdust/wood shavings. The most important thing is to get to the spill quickly.

Once the bulk of the mess is removed, you may still have an oil stain. If the stain is in an area where any liquid run-off will go into the waterways, you need to be very careful about the products you use to remove it. A small area may be cleaned simply by pouring a can of energy drink over it and scrubbing with an outdoor broom. Use an old towel to soak up the residue and then leave to dry.

Dispose of the towel responsibly. Don't wash it in your washing machine, as the oil residue may damage the machine.

More stubborn stains may require hydrochloric acid (be careful on painted concrete) or a heavy-duty degreaser. For either of these, you can apply the product to the area and use a stiff broom to work the product in to remove the stain. Use an old towel to remove the excess. (These types of products are available at Bunnings, AutoBarn and Supercheap Auto stores. Again, be careful with liquid run-off and follow the instructions on these products carefully.)

Sawdust

Vacuum with a heavy-duty vacuum (sometimes called a shop vacuum/vac, or a workshop vacuum). These are available relatively cheaply from outlets like Bunnings, and are able to deal with heavy-duty debris that may damage a residential vacuum. These vacuums are a good investment if you regularly use your garage for woodwork projects or similar. They are also great for outside.

If you don't have a heavy-duty vacuum, you can simply sweep the sawdust into a pile and use a dustpan to collect it for the bin.

If you have the space for storage, it's a great idea to grab a bucket with a lid from Bunnings and keep your sawdust in there. You can then use it for any oil or petrol spills that may occur.

Rachael's *tip*

If the shavings are from untreated timber, you can also compost them.

Paint spills

Get to the spill as soon as you can. Soak up what you can with an old towel or paper towels. Pop the towel/paper in a bag once you are finished to avoid the paint spreading.

If the paint is water based, a good scrub with a stiff-bristle brush and soapy water will likely be enough, even on a porous surface.

For an oil-based paint you will need to use a solvent like turpentine (turps). If you need to use turps, ensure you take adequate safety precautions: wear gloves and a mask, and ensure you have good ventilation in the area. Use the same method of scrubbing with a stiff-bristle brush as you would for water-based paint, then tip the turps onto the area. Avoid the waste entering the stormwater drains by soaking it up with paper or old towels and disposing of them appropriately.

Grass stains from the lawnmower

Hot soapy water and a stiff outdoor broom are all you need to remove grass stains. Dip the broom into the soapy water and scrub over the grass stains.

Petrol and two-stroke fuel spills

First, ensure there are no open flames in the area. Then put on a pair of gloves and a mask, and ensure the area is well ventilated.

You now need to soak up the liquid. As with oil, you can use kitty litter, flour or sawdust/wood shavings. Cover the spill and leave for 30 minutes, then sweep the absorbent product into a garbage bag. Throw the garbage bag away where there is zero chance of anything burning being thrown on top of it or near it.

Use hot soapy water to scrub the area and leave to dry while well ventilated.

If you do a lot of mechanical work in your garage, you may like to invest in a spill kit. These can make clean-up safer for everyone and ensure that pollutants don't end up in our waterways. You can purchase spill kits from Bunnings and safety-equipment shops like RSEA.

outdoor
entertaining/
balcony

create a relaxing space

with minimal effort

IT CAN BE CHALLENGING TO KEEP an outdoor entertaining or relaxation area clean. Dust, mildew, dirt, pet hair and plant debris are all difficult to keep at bay. But, as with any other part of the home, regular maintenance can save you a lot of energy in the long run.

The regular tasks you need to complete are part of the General Cleaning chapter. Cobwebs and dusting should be your main focus – don't forget any kids' play equipment. If you keep up with these tasks, the area will remain looking pretty great. If you have lots of trees around you, add sweeping up leaf litter (or using a garden blower) to those general cleaning tasks.

Outdoor Surfaces

OUTDOOR SURFACES CAN BE TRICKY to clean as they are not usually smooth (to allow for grip). Avoid fabric mops as the fibres will stick to the texture of the tile, making the surface hard to clean and even making it look worse.

In a bucket, combine hot water and 1 cup of vinegar. If you have grease or grime, you can add a small squirt of dishwashing liquid. Dip a stiff broom (like an outdoor broom or a deck scrubber) into the solution and scrub the tiles, moving backwards and forwards. You may like to pour the solution onto the tiles to make the task a little easier.

If you have a pressure washer, you can use that instead. Some models sell additional attachments for outdoor flooring that might make it even easier.

If your flooring is becoming mildewed, you might like to use a product such as 30 Seconds Outdoor Cleaner, available at Bunnings, which is suitable for removing mildew from a range of surfaces. White vinegar may also help, but isn't suitable for all floors as it's acidic (you cannot use it on some natural stone pavers, for example). Make sure you follow the available guidelines for your particular flooring material.

Decking

A SPRAY MOP IS A GREAT WAY to clean decking that's in good condition. A quick once-over when it's getting a bit dirty or dusty will keep your outdoor relaxation area a haven. Water is all you need for an everyday clean.

Decking requires a good scrub and oil every so often. How often you do this will depend on the deck's exposure to the elements. Bunnings sell a great deck-cleaning product called Cabot's Deck Clean, and oil is available from any store that sells paint.

Pet Odours

OUTDOOR AREAS CAN OFTEN START SMELLING a bit like your pets. If the odour is just a general one (not urine), then a vinegar wash over the flooring surface will neutralise it.

White vinegar, although helpful, isn't suitable for all floor types as it's acidic. Make sure you follow the guidelines for your particular flooring material.

Spray any cushions with Pet Odour Eliminator (see Odour-eliminating Recipes) – just a misting – and allow it to dry. The spray will neutralise the odour.

If your area smells heavily of animal urine and a floor-clean doesn't remove it, you can use a urine scent-elimination product such as Piss Off! Odour Absorber, or the TRUEECO Dog and Cat Urine Eliminator to tackle the problem areas.

Outdoor Furniture
· · · · · · · · · · · · · · · · · ·

Glass table

First, remove dust with a dusting cloth. For any stubborn or sticky marks, spray with a general-purpose cleaner and mist over the rest of the table. Use a glass-cleaning cloth to clean and polish as you go, covering the whole area. Don't forget the underside, especially if the table is clear.

Timber table

Use a dry brush (such as the one from a dustpan set) to brush the table well, including underneath. Spot-clean any marks using a cloth sprayed with general-purpose cleaner.

Be sure to oil your table regularly to keep the surface in top condition.

Aluminium table

Brush down with a soft brush and wipe over with a damp cloth. You can use a general-purpose cleaner if there are any marks.

Wicker furniture

It may seem surprising but wicker is a really hardy material for your outdoor furniture. Providing it is in good condition, you can simply brush down the wicker with a soft brush and hose it off. Leave the pieces in a well-ventilated area to dry fully. If you prefer, you can use a bucket of soapy water and a cloth to clean the piece.

If your wicker is quite dirty you might like to use a dish brush with bristles instead of a cloth. This type of brush will really get into the grooves of the weave and leave you with a very clean surface.

Cushions

For a general clean, shake the cushion vigorously, then use water or an upholstery cleaner for any stains/marks. Water will likely be enough in most cases, but you might like to spray with a 4:1 mixture of water to vinegar, with a dash of dishwashing liquid. For very stubborn areas, use a soft-bristle brush to scrub the area.

Some outdoor furniture cushions can also be pressure-washed. Place them on some grass and spray evenly over the surface. Leave to dry on a flat, well-drained surface.

If you find your cushions have mould or mildew forming on them, use straight white vinegar to spray over the area and allow it to soak for 30–60 minutes. Scrub with a medium-bristle brush and wipe clean with a cloth.

Barbecue

CLEANING YOUR BARBECUE ALWAYS SEEMS like a hard task – they always tend to look really grimy. Regular maintenance and cleaning, however, will keep the barbecue looking nice, make it easier to clean each time, and make using the barbecue more appealing.

Hotplates and grill

After cooking, sprinkle some table salt or cooking salt onto the warm hotplate. Then, using the cut side of half a lemon, rub the salt over the hotplate. Wipe up with an old cloth or paper towels.

A grill brush is very helpful for the grill. Avoid the bristle brushes and go for the bristle-free coil type of brush. The bristle brushes can lose small bristles while cleaning and create a hazard if they lodge in food the next time you cook.

For a deep clean, remove the hotplates and grill plates from the barbecue housing. Spray the plates with a degreaser (BBQ Magic Cleaner and Degreaser is a great option). Wipe over with newspaper or rags. You can even pressure-wash them if they are heavily soiled.

Stainless steel exterior

For a general clean, you can use a stainless steel cleaner and a cloth to wipe over the surface. A dry cloth gives the best results.

If your barbecue's surface has rust-like marks, Bar Keepers Friend Cleanser & Polish Powder does an excellent job of bringing it back to life. Get a little pot of water and a damp cloth. Sprinkle some powder onto the damp cloth and start rubbing over the stainless steel surfaces. Dip the cloth in water regularly to keep the area fairly wet but not dripping. Add more powder as required. Once the area is cleaned, wipe over with a clean dampened cloth to remove any residue. Dry with a dry cloth or towel.

Coated exterior

Painted or powder-coated barbecues can be cleaned simply with a general-purpose cleaner and a cloth. Spray the surface and wipe after a minute or two to let the cleaner work on any grease that might be sitting on the surface, making it easier to wipe off.

Outdoor Fridge

WIPE OVER WITH A STAINLESS STEEL and glass cleaner solution (see Cleaning Recipes) and a microfibre cloth. Be sure to do the inside of the fridge with the same solution. If your fridge has a lot of condensation, use a towel to mop that up first so you're starting with a fairly dry surface.

Outdoor Fan

OUTDOOR FANS CAN BECOME covered in cobwebs and dust. Regular cleaning will make this job easier and keep your fans in top working condition.

Ceiling fan

Ensure the fan is switched off.

Use a cobweb broom to remove cobwebs and as much dust from the top of the blades as possible. Use a stepladder to access the top of the blade and wipe with a damp cloth and general-purpose spray.

Wall fan

Turn off the power to the fan before starting any cleaning.

Remove the front housing from the fan. Wipe each fan blade section with a cloth sprayed with general-purpose cleaner. Immerse the housing in a bucket of soapy water and agitate. Leave to dry on a towel. Do not reconnect until the housing is totally dry.

If you can remove the rear housing, do this too. If not, use a damp cloth to wipe each part. This can be a little tedious but is the best way to get to each section.

Use a clean cloth sprayed with general-purpose spray to wipe over the rest of the fan unit.

If you have an air blow gun attached to an air compressor, a can of compressed air or a garden blower, you can use that to blast the dust off the fan if the build-up isn't too difficult to remove.

Blinds *and* Screens
· · · · · · · · · · · · · · · · ·

PVC blinds

Use a wet cloth to remove soiling such as bird droppings or mud splashes. Take care not to scratch the surface when wiping. Cleaning these types of messes as they occur is the best method to maintain the scratch-free finish on your blinds.

Many manufacturers recommend using VuPlex Plastic Cleaner (available at Bunnings and elsewhere). Apply the VuPlex to the blind and use a cotton cloth to slowly and gently wipe the product over the blind. The cloth will start absorbing the product, and with it the dirt. It's important to use a cotton cloth to avoid scratching the blind.

As well as cleaning your PVC blinds, VuPlex is also designed to protect them from yellowing and sticking, and it can prolong their life.

Don't use harsh cleaners on your blinds (methylated spirits, alcohol, etc.) as they can damage the surface.

Apply a silicone spray to the blind's zips or tracks every so often to lubricate them and ensure they function well and to prolong their lifespan.

Sunscreen roller blinds

Remove heavy messes like bird droppings and mud as soon as possible to keep your blinds in top condition. Use a cloth dampened with cold soapy water to spot-clean these marks. Avoid pushing too hard as it may distort the shape. Use a cobweb broom to remove all cobwebs and as much dust as possible. Spray the blind with cold soapy water (a mild dishwashing liquid works well). Wipe over the blind on each side to remove the dust and dirt. Hose the mixture off when complete (or use a wet cloth to wipe over again).

Ensure the blind is fully dry before rolling it up. Leaving them down as much as possible is usually recommended to avoid roller distortion.

Don't use any harsh products like methylated spirits or Windex. Pressure washers may also damage the blind.

Canvas awnings

Use a soft brush to clean the debris off both inside and outside the awning, then hose down with clean water.

If you find mould or mildew, you can use the 30 Seconds Outdoor Cleaner from Bunnings to remove this. Check the manufacturer's instructions before cleaning.

yard

*simple ways to keep your
garden tidy (even if you're
not a gardener)*

STREET APPEAL IS REALLY IMPORTANT as it sets the tone for your home. If you have a front yard, you will see it when you come home, and arriving home to a mess isn't likely to put you in, or sustain, a great mood. If you do your own gardening, try to allocate an hour a month to weeding or spraying and tidying the garden beds, and mow lawns fortnightly to maintain your grass. If you do these tasks regularly, it doesn't take much effort.

Lawns, Gardens *and* Paths

SET YOURSELF A REGULAR LAWN-MOWING DAY if you can. This will give you a routine for picking up toys, dog mess and any other mess in the yard. Once a month, add in the weeding and every so often add in some pruning time. You don't need to be a green thumb – if you keep on top of these tasks, your garden will thrive.

If you have synthetic lawn, make sure you keep up with spraying weeds and vacuuming or blowing off the debris. If you have lots of trees, you may need to do this weekly; otherwise, monthly upkeep should be enough.

Once your lawn and garden are under control, concentrate on keeping your paths clear of bark, stones and dirt. Sweeping with an outdoor broom is easy and can be done at any time of the day. If you prefer, you can use a garden blower to complete the task with minimal effort. Sweep or blow all the debris into a corner or pile and discard it (or pop it back in the garden).

Gutters

GUTTER CLEANING IS SO IMPORTANT. Taking care of your gutters is the best way to prevent storm damage caused by rain. Keeping debris out of your gutters ensures they drain well when it rains, and it prolongs the life of the gutters themselves. If debris sits in the gutters and traps water, your gutters will begin to rust.

If you live in an area with lots of trees you may find you need to clean your gutters weekly or fortnightly. In other areas, yearly cleaning might be enough. Gutter cleaning is fairly easy and doesn't require a lot of skill, so it can be a do-it-yourself task. However, you should take into account your physical abilities and steadiness. If you aren't very steady or fall easily, it's best to enlist help from a friend, handyman or plumber.

Your roof style will dictate what equipment you need. For most single-storey homes, you just require a ladder, gloves and a bucket. Climb the ladder so that you can easily reach inside the gutter. Using your hands or an appropriately sized scoop, remove the debris and place it in the bucket. As the bucket fills, empty it into your garden waste bin or compost bin. Continue until all areas are clear.

Do not clean your gutters in wet or windy weather.

Drains

EVERY SO OFTEN, WHEN IT RAINS, take a look at your outdoor drains and make sure the water is going down quickly. If the water is moving slowly, you may find that your drains are filling with leaf litter or other debris. Most drains will have a grate you can remove to scoop out the debris. If the blockage persists, you may need a plumber to take a look.

Bins

COUNCIL BINS CAN GET MANKY pretty quickly. Giving them a clean every so often will make taking the bins out a slightly more appealing task (or at least less unappealing!).

After your bins have been emptied, put a generous squirt of dishwashing liquid into the bottom and add some water (hot if you can, but cold is okay). If you have a build-up at the bottom, let it soak for 5–10 minutes. Use a small, stiff broom to scrub the inside of the bin and around the lip. Lay the bin down to empty the water and then use a cloth and general-purpose spray to wipe the outside and handles down. Tip the bin upside down and leave the lid open to dry effectively.

Karlie's *tip*

A pressure washer can make this task much quicker and easier.

Letterbox

LETTERBOXES ARE OFTEN OVERLOOKED in cleaning but every now and then it's a great idea to wipe them over. If your letterbox has any metal parts, it may have some rust spots to deal with.

Start by removing any cobwebs (and checking for spiders – eek!). If you have rust spots, use some Bar Keepers Friend Cleanser & Polish Powder to remove them. Start with a wet cloth and sprinkle a little powder onto it. Use circular motions on the metal areas to restore them to their former glory. Wipe over with a clean wet cloth to

remove the residue. Spray the inside with a general-purpose spray and wipe out. Give the rest of the letterbox a wipe down.

Air Conditioning Units

THE CONDENSER UNIT of your air conditioner may be on the outside of your home. Take a minute every so often to ensure there is no grass growing into the unit and no leaf litter stuck to it. You can also take this time to give the solid parts a wipe over with a general-purpose spray and a cloth.

Water *and* Gas Meters

YOU SHOULD ALWAYS MAKE SURE your meters are clear of debris so they are easy to read – this means you will be less likely to have a billing issue. Every few months take a quick look and remove any leaf litter or rubbish that has accumulated around the meters. Ensure nothing is left in the way that might make the meters more difficult to read.

Outdoor Lighting

ENSURE YOUR LIGHTS ARE TURNED OFF, then remove cobwebs and wipe quickly with a damp cloth. This is usually all that is required. Some models may get insects caught inside. If this is the case you can usually unscrew the cover (make sure the light is switched off) and wipe the insects out. Check all the globes and replace any that aren't working (or pop them on your shopping list). Then replace the cover.

Plant Pots

DAMPEN A CLOTH WITH GENERAL-PURPOSE spray and wipe over all glazed and non-porous pots. For porous pots, a small brush from a dustpan is a better option to remove dust and dirt.

aromas
for
your
home

amazing ways to trick people

into thinking your home

is cleaner than it is

A DELICIOUS SCENT IN THE AIR CAN trick you into believing an area is cleaner than it is. Some people have been known to spray their front doors with a scent so that their visitors have a 'clean feeling' before even stepping inside! (Sneaky or genius?)

Scent can be a really important factor in the feeling of a clean and comfortable home. Unfortunately, bad smells infiltrate more easily than lovely ones. Use these tips to combat bad smells and introduce great scents to your home.

Tools *for* Combating Odour
· · · · · · · · · · · · · · · · ·

AS WITH YOUR REGULAR CLEANING, having great tools for dealing with odours makes the task easier – and they might even help you keep on top of it.

Candles

Scented candles are a great way to create lovely scents in your home. Lighting a candle after cleaning your home creates a sense that the job is done.

Ensure that you are careful with candles. Never place them near curtains or other flammable materials and never leave them unattended around young children and pets, as they can be a fire hazard. Always make sure that they have been blown out before leaving the house or going to sleep.

Wax melts

Wax melts work in a similar way to candles. You'll need a wax warmer to warm the wax and release the scent. There are electric models, and others that use tea light candles.

Diffusers

Diffusers are a great way to spread a nice aroma throughout your home.

Electric

These diffusers use a combination of water and your chosen essential oil to create a scented mist. They come in many different designs, and can often serve as decorative items too.

Natural

These diffusers are made from natural materials like banksia pods and reeds. The natural fibres soak up and diffuse the scent.

Incense

Incense is made from aromatic plant materials and scented with essential oils. The incense is lit with a flame then smoulders, releasing a fragrant smell.

Take care when using incense as it can be a fire hazard if left unattended. Never place lit incense near curtains or other flammable materials.

Potpourri

Dried potpourri

Traditional dried potpourri is made from flowers and spices, and comes in a range of looks and fragrances. Simply sit it in a decorative bowl in the room of your choice. You can get specialised decorative containers for dry potpourri, which have lids to limit the dust that settles on it.

Stovetop potpourri

Stovetop potpourri is a great way to spread a natural scent through your home. Combine your favourite spices and some citrus peel with water and boil gently on the stove.

Room sprays

Room sprays are a nice way to quickly add fragrance to a room. They are simple to use – just spray little bursts of scent as you walk around your home.

Fabric sprays

Fabric sprays are very similar to room sprays but they are designed specifically for fabrics. You can use these on clothing, linens, cushions, throws, curtains, and upholstered items (e.g. couches, occasional chairs).

Carpet deodorisers

Powder

Carpet deodorisers come in a few different forms. The most popular is a powder that you sprinkle on your carpet. Some require brushing to work the powder into the fibres; others are simply sprinkled on top of the carpet. You then vacuum the powder up, leaving a pleasant scent.

Aerosol/foam

Foam or aerosol carpet deodorisers are simply sprayed onto the carpet and left to dry. No Vac is probably the most popular brand in Mums Who Clean.

Air purifiers and dehumidifiers

Air purifiers and dehumidifiers remove bad odours from the air rather than just covering them up. They are great for homes with limited ventilation.

Air purifiers

These machines come in many forms. Some are purely air purifiers, while others perform several functions. These multipurpose machines can be quite useful, as air purifiers can take up a lot of space. The Dyson Pure Hot+Cool is a great multipurpose machine: it is a heater, fan and air purifier all in one.

Dehumidifiers

Dehumidifiers are machines that recirculate air after removing the moisture from it. They can be especially helpful in older homes that have dampness issues or the smell of dampness.

Plants

Bringing plants into your home is a great way to improve its overall feel and scent.

Potted

Potted plants add great colour to a home, as well as adding a fresh and earthy fragrance.

Fresh flowers

Fresh flowers add a beautiful and natural scent to your home. Be sure to remove the stamens (the pollen-loaded parts) from lilies or similar flowers. When the stamens fall, they will leave hard-to-remove yellow stains on anything they touch. To remove the stamens, cover your fingers with a tissue and grab each one. (Some flowers, while natural, can be toxic to humans and pets.)

Scent packs

Scent packs are small fabric bags that contain scented material such as plastic beads, dried plant leaves or dried flowers. These are great for throwing into drawers, cupboards, shoes and bags.

Essential oils

Essential oils are extracted from plants and can be used in many ways to deal with odours:

- **Add them to some cleaning solutions for scent (and cleaning power).**
- **Use them in a diffuser to spread scent through your home.**

- **Add a few drops in with your laundry detergent (alternatively add it to some vinegar in the fabric softener compartment) to give your clothing and other items a great scent.**

Note

Essential oils, while natural, can be toxic to both humans and pets. If you are unsure, you should consult a doctor, pharmacist or accredited aromatherapist to ensure the oils you are choosing are safe for your family, including any pets.

Essential oils can be pure – just one scent – or blended from several scents. Each oil and blend has its own unique fragrance, so go into a store if you can and sniff out your favourites. Use good-quality oils – they are easy to obtain and don't need to cost the earth. You can buy them from chemists or aromatherapists in person or, if you already know what you love, you can try online retailers such as ECO Modern Essentials.

Fighting Specific Odours

Funky fridge

Place a small bowl of bicarb in the back of the fridge. Replace once a month. If the smell lingers after a day or two, make sure there is no expired food in the fridge. Then clean the fridge thoroughly (see Kitchen chapter).

Terrible toilet

Sprinkle bicarb over the floor around the toilet and into the bowl. Cut a lemon into quarters. Squeeze lemon juice over the bicarb, then add the lemon quarters to the toilet bowl. Leave for a few hours. Remove the lemon and flush. Vacuum up the bicarb from the floor (ensuring you do not vacuum any liquid).

You can also use shaving foam to remove bad odours around/in your toilet. Smother the toilet and floor around it in shaving foam. Leave for a few hours, then wipe up with a warm, damp cloth or mop.

Whiffy washing machine

Starting with an empty washing machine, add a few spoonfuls of bicarb to the detergent drawer, and a splash of vinegar in the machine drum. Run a hot wash cycle.

If you prefer to use liquids, you can pour white vinegar into your fabric softener drawer and add 2-3 drops of lavender essential oil before running a hot wash cycle.

Horrible hands

Lots of different cooking ingredients can make your hands smell horrible. Onion, garlic and fish are three of the main offenders. To deal with this, cut a lemon in half and thoroughly rub your hands with it. Rub your hands with hand sanitiser and the smell will be gone.

Another option to help with smell is rubbing your hands on a metal spoon or your sink! It sounds strange, but many people find that stainless steel really does help. Others find that milk is a great odour eliminator for cooking hands. Just pour milk onto your hands and rub well, then wash the milk off with your usual hand soap.

Cruddy carpet

Use a commercial or homemade carpet deodoriser powder or foam, following the package instructions. Alternatively, sprinkle the carpet with bicarb. Leave it to absorb the odour for a few hours or overnight, then vacuum up as normal.

Rank rubbish bin

Sprinkle your bin with bicarb and leave in the sun for a few hours. Rinse out. Sprinkle a little bicarb or 1-2 drops of essential oil in the base of the bin before you add your new bin bag.

Smelly sink

Remove the plug and sprinkle your sink with bicarb, and pour 1 cup of vinegar over the top. Leave to bubble and froth for a few minutes. Boil your kettle and pour the boiling water over the top. The sink will be shiny and the drain will have had a lovely clean.

Sofa stench

You can deodorise your couch in a similar way to the carpet. Sprinkle with bicarb, leave for a few hours and vacuum up. If you have removable covers on your couch cushions, take a little scent pack or a cloth sprayed with essential oil, open the cover, pop the scent pack or cloth in with the couch cushion and close the cover again.

Pet pong

Pet odours can be tricky as we can't always detect them ourselves. Cleaning your soft furnishings regularly, including curtains, cushions, couches, linens and pet bedding, can help remove odours from your home.

Deep-cleaning carpets is best but between cleans you might like to use a pet odour spray such as No Vac Foaming Sanitiser and Deodoriser Fresh Pet, or you can use the Pet Odour Eliminator from our Odour Eliminating Recipes section.

Stinky shoes

Sprinkle bicarb inside shoes and leave them in the sun. Vacuum out and they will be stink free.

You can also mist the fabric parts of the shoes with dry shampoo to remove bad odours. Between uses, pop a scent pack inside each shoe to keep odours at bay.

my
home
is out of
control

simple steps to getting

on top of a messy house

IT'S SO EASY TO GET INTO A RUT and let your home get out of control. When it becomes a mess, you may find yourself overwhelmed – and swamped with panic when you have surprise visitors arriving in thirty minutes' time!

A busy lifestyle, an illness or a change of schedule are all times when cleaning and tidying can become less of a priority. This is really common and completely normal – you're not the only one experiencing this.

If you have no idea where to start, then start here! This basic list, arranged in order, will simplify the task before you, make it feel more manageable, and help you get your whole home cleaned. It might be just what you need to get going.

This list will get your home back to a respectable standard, so that you're ready to move on to a deep clean. Complete the steps in the order they appear in for the quickest results. Chuck on the Mums Who Get It Done Spotify playlist to keep yourself on track and motivated.

Rubbish

• • • • • • • • • • • • • • • • •

PICK UP ALL RUBBISH in your home and take it to your outside bins.

Carry a garbage bag or tub with you the whole way around your home and pick up every little scrap of waste. Common areas that are forgotten are the bedrooms (used tissues), the bathroom (empty bottles and toilet-paper rolls) and the toy room/playroom (empty packets and bags).

Washing

PICK UP ALL DIRTY CLOTHES and linen and put them in the laundry – in a hamper, or just on the floor. Put a load on now. If you have lots to do, use short/ quick cycles to get back into the swing of it. Change the loads as you go on with your cleaning. Consider using a dryer for these loads to speed up the process.

If you already have clean washing ready to put away, make your bed now and place it all on the bed. On a day like this, it is helpful to put it all in one place to sort later. Don't go to bed before this is done, though, or it just becomes a bigger issue.

Dishes

COLLECT ALL DISHES FROM AROUND YOUR HOME. Wash a load or stack the dishwasher. Do more loads if required as you go on with your cleaning.

Be sure to check bedside tables and in kids' and teenagers' rooms.

If you have heaps of items for handwashing, it might be helpful to pop a towel over the stove and leave the dishes there to dry while you complete other tasks. This way you are not restricted by the limited size of your draining area.

Tidying

PICK UP EVERY ITEM THAT IS NOT where it belongs. Put it in its home. If you don't know where it lives, find a box/basket/hamper and designate it your 'crap box'. Put all the stuff you can't rehome in here and deal with it later. This helps you keep on task and not get bogged down in details.

If you have space in a wardrobe or similar, pop the crap box in there so it's out of the way for now.

Rachael's *tip*

Pop a note in your planner or calendar to ensure you don't forget about your crap box.

Toilet

PUT SOME TOILET CLEANER IN the toilet bowl and leave it to do its work.

Cobwebs

GRAB A COBWEB BROOM AND BRUSH over your cornices, doorjambs and corners.

Dusting

DO A BASIC DUST of window frames, wall hangings and surfaces/furniture. An extendable duster makes this job easier; however, any dry cloth will get the job done.

Surfaces *and* Bathroom

USE A GENERAL-PURPOSE SPRAY to clean your surfaces and furniture. Wipe down with a microfibre cloth as you go. Do your bathroom at this step – just a wipe over. Finish off by brushing and flushing the toilet.

Vacuuming

DO A BASIC VACUUM OF THE WHOLE HOME, including hard floors. A stick vacuum is sufficient if you have one – no need to get your big one out.

Mopping

MOP YOUR HARD SURFACES. (If you have an all-in-one vacuum/mop like a CrossWave or HIZERO, use this on your hard floors instead of vacuuming them separately.)

Remember that this is just a basic clean, not an in-depth clean, and you can do it in a short amount of time. If you are pressed for time, you might like to set a timer to rush through it.

Once you have completed the basic clean, you can work through the rooms in this book to complete your deep clean in a more leisurely fashion.

Rachael's *tip*

Multitask while vacuuming or mopping – add scent to your mop water or vacuum filter. The scent will spread through the house while you work.

unexpected
guests

quick tips for taking the stress

out of last-minute visitors

IF SOMEONE CALLS TO LET YOU KNOW that they are popping by in twenty minutes, it might send you into a tizzy! The important thing to remember is that social guests are coming to see *you* – not to inspect your home. Try to focus on that!

If you think you'd like to have a slightly cleaner home, though, focus on these ten quick-cleaning tasks to make your home look and feel pretty good.

1. Pop on your diffuser or light a scented candle.
2. Stack the dishwasher. (Or shove the dirty dishes in the oven to hide them!)
3. Pick up any rubbish.
4. Throw any clothes lying around your home into the laundry or hampers.
5. Vacuum the floors in the main areas.
6. Spot-clean any noticeable spots on hard floors – you won't have time to mop.
7. Check the toilet and handwashing area and wipe down if necessary.
8. Shut bedroom doors or doors to any areas that don't need to be seen.
9. Wipe the benchtop or table where you're likely to sit.
10. Pop the kettle on and enjoy your time with your guests.

cleaning your cleaning tools

how to keep your cleaning
tools in top working order

CLEANING YOUR CLEANING TOOLS is an important part of keeping your home clean. If your tools are not maintained correctly they may lose their effectiveness – and even become damaged.

The manual will tell you how to clean your model, but the steps below may help too.

Broom

· · · · · · · · · · · · · · · · · ·

CLEANING A BROOM IS USUALLY AS SIMPLE as wiping the bristles to remove any dust or build-up, rinsing them in a sink with warm water and leaving out to dry.

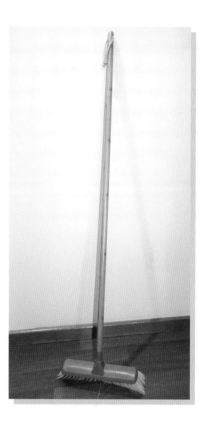

Brushes

· · · · · · · · · · · · · · · · ·

HOW YOU CLEAN YOUR BRUSHES – including any toothbrushes you have used for cleaning – will depend on what you have used them for.

First, remove any stuck-in particles. Then, if they need a deeper clean, fill a cup with disinfectant or vinegar. Place the brush into the cup with the bristles facing down and leave to soak for 20 minutes, then pop in the sun to dry.

Cobweb Broom

CLEANING A COBWEB BROOM is very simple. You can rinse it under water or simply pop on some gloves and remove any tangled webs.

Duster

DUSTERS DO EXACTLY what they are meant to do: collect dust. The easiest way to remove this dust from your duster is with a sticky lint roller. Rolling this up and down the duster will remove the dust, leaving it clean and ready for its next job.

Some dusters can be handwashed with warm soapy water or even put into the washing machine.

Dustpan *and* Brush

YOUR DUSTPAN AND BRUSH can be cleaned in a similar way to your broom. Remove any dust or build-up, then rinse with warm water.

Kitchen Sponges

· · · · · · · · · · · · · · · ·

THERE ARE A FEW DIFFERENT TYPES of kitchen sponges and most are meant to be reused multiple times.

To keep them clean and free of germs, pop them in the dishwasher at the end of the night. If you can, have a few in rotation so you can leave the freshly washed one on your dish rack to air-dry.

Some sponges, such as the White Magic Washing Up Pad, are able to be washed in the washing machine.

HIZERO

· · · · · · · · · · · · · · · ·

FOR DAILY MAINTENANCE AFTER USE, empty the clean and waste water tanks. Refill the clean water tank. Open the brush roller cover and empty the solid waste tray. Replace and close the cover. Ensure that power to the base is not switched on. Place the machine on the base and run a cleaning cycle. Once completed, empty both tanks and cleaning is done.

For weekly maintenance or if you notice water spots being left on your floor, you need to complete a deep clean on the machine. Remove the clean and waste water tanks, rinse with clean water and set aside to dry.

Open the roller cover and remove the brush roller, remove the debris on the roller by hand and rinse in clean water. Then set aside to dry. Remove the solid waste container and rinse with clean water. Set aside to dry. Close the brush cover and turn the machine on its side. You can do this on a table or the floor. Access the underneath of the machine and remove the roller and use a cloth to wipe away any build-up in the machine. Remove the sink drain, rinse under water and set aside to dry.

Once all parts are dry (except the roller) you can put your machine back together.

Microfibre Cloths

· · · · · · · · · · · · · · · · ·

MOST CLOTHS CAN BE POPPED IN the washing machine on a normal cycle. After a while they will start to look a bit old and mucky. This is a great time to do a boil wash.

Boil a pot of water on the cooktop, add the cloths and boil until the water becomes dirty (around 10 minutes).

Leave to cool and then remove them from the water. Pop through a standard washing machine cycle and hang out to dry.

Screen-cleaning Cloths

· · · · · · · · · · · · · · · · ·

THESE ARE ALSO VERY EASY TO WASH. You can give them a rinse, or wash with soapy water. They are a bit more delicate than microfibre cloths so putting them through the washing machine is not recommended.

Sponges

HOW YOU WASH YOUR SPONGE will depend on what you have cleaned with it and how dirty your sponge is.

If you have used a sponge to clean your benchtops or sink, you can wash it in warm soapy water or in a wash with disinfectant.

If you have used your sponge to clean your toilet, you will definitely want to disinfect it. Pop it in a tub of water and disinfectant, or in a tub of vinegar and water. Leave to soak for a few hours and then hang it in the sun to dry.

Spray Bottles

SOMETIMES SPRAY BOTTLES CAN GET CLOGGED. The best way to clear the nozzle is to soak it in warm water and then try to pump some warm water through. This usually clears any blockages and fixes the problem. If the tip of the nozzle is still clogged, try using a pin to clear it.

Giving your bottles a quick wipe over after use will make sure that they don't get sticky or gunky.

Spray Mop

SPRAY MOPS ARE EXTREMELY EASY to clean. Most have a pad that is attached to the bottom with elastic or velcro. You can remove this pad easily, then handwash or pop it in the washing machine.

The liquid canister can be rinsed with warm water and left out to dry. The handle and stick can be wiped down with a cloth.

Vacuum/Mop

HOW YOU CLEAN YOUR VACUUM will depend on the type of vacuum you have. The instruction manual will advise you on the best way to clean your specific model.

Doing a quick clean, however, is fairly similar for all models. Most vacuums have three main parts that you can clean on a regular basis: the barrel, the stick and the head.

Cleaning the barrel is usually as simple as removing the trap and emptying out the contents. Some barrels can be removed completely so that you can give them a wash with warm water. Check your manual before doing this.

The stick itself just needs to be checked for blockages. Have a look and see if you can see any obstructions. If you can, these can usually be removed by giving the stick a shake or a tap. If not, check your manual for advice on how to dislodge a blockage or build-up.

The head of the vacuum attracts all sorts of things that need to be cleaned off – sticky substances that you need to wipe off, or trapped hair, lint or dust in the brush. Your manual will give instructions on how to remove the brush for a thorough clean. Usually a comb, or your hand with a wet glove, is enough to remove this debris.

Your filter will also need cleaning, but methods differ. Please check your manual.

Bissell CrossWave Cordless

To clean a CrossWave, use the 3-in-1 docking station. Put your machine on the station and pour water into the rinse funnel on the back. Push the Clean Out Cycle button and hold down for about 15 seconds. (If you have a corded version, you need to tip the handle back and turn the machine on to activate the roller.)

Next, remove the brush roll cover by pulling it upward. While not necessary, you can rinse this under water again to make sure it is super clean. Pop aside to dry.

Remove the brush roll and rinse with warm water, then place it into the drying tray to dry. Dry the inside of the brush roll area. Once dry, you can replace the brush roll – right side first – then click the press-down tab on the left to lock it into place.

Replace the brush roll cover by lining it back up with the edges of the base and pushing it back until it clicks in.

Remove the cleaning tank and discard the fluid. Rinse the tank and leave to dry.

Remove the dirty water tank by pushing down the recessed button and pull the handle away from the machine. Remove the top of the tank and the strainer. Pour the water down the sink and rinse out any remaining gunk. Remove the filter and rinse under warm water. You can use a mild soap if you like. Leave on a benchtop to dry.

Wipe out the area where the dirty water tank attaches to the machine.

Once all parts are dry you can put your machine back together. Replace the filter, then the strainer, followed by the top of the tank. Place the assembled tank back into the machine.

Bissell ProHeat 2X Revolution Pet

The ProHeat is a fantastic cleaning machine that has so many uses. It is also very easy to clean.

Place the ProHeat into the cleaning tray and open the accessory flap (on top of the machine). Use the measuring jug to fill the cleaning tray with water. Turn the machine on to activate the rollers. After around 8 seconds, close the accessory flap. This will allow the machine to suck up all the dirty water.

Remove the clean water tank, empty and allow it to dry.

Remove the dirty water tank. Pull the rubber tab at the top of the tank. Tilt it to pour out the dirty water. Rinse the tank with clean water and then close the rubber tab. Unscrew the ring at the base of the tank. Remove the float carefully and rinse. The float will lock back into place and you can then replace the ring. Make sure you do it up tightly or it may leak. Set this aside to dry.

Remove the nozzle brush by pulling up towards you gently. Next, remove the brush roll cover. Press the release buttons and lift up. Rinse the nozzle and brush roll cover under warm water. Use the nozzle cleaning tool to remove any debris. Pop them aside to dry.

Comb the brush roll. Return the dried brush roll cover and nozzle to the machine.

Bissell SpotClean

Cleaning your SpotClean machine is very easy. Your instruction manual will have a detailed description of how to do this.

Once you have finished cleaning your item, fill your sink or a bowl with some water. Use the SpotClean to suck up the water to clean the hose and tool. Remove the cleaning tank and discard the fluid. Rinse the tank and leave to dry.

Remove your dirty water tank and, over a sink, unlock and remove the lid, pour out the water and rinse out any remaining gunk. Leave to dry, reassemble and pop back on your machine.

Angle the hose so that any remaining water can drain. Then roll it back up and remove the tool attached. Rinse the tool under clean running water and set aside to dry.

real-estate cleaning

essential cleaning advice

for a smooth and stress-free

house move or inspection

Vacate/End of Lease Cleaning

· · · · · · · · · · · · · · · · ·

MOVING OUT OF A RENTAL PROPERTY can be really confusing and stressful if it's not something you do often. Use these steps to ensure the cleaning of your rental home is up to standard.

What you need

Having everything on hand before you begin will make the cleaning process efficient and streamlined. The amount of time each task will take will differ depending on the size and condition of the home you are cleaning.

The kits listed below have items that cross over. There's no need to buy two or more of these – you can reuse them at every step.

Basic Cleaning Kit

This is best stored all together in a caddy, basket or bucket that you can take from room to room. It should include:

- several microfibre cloths – standard ones (e.g. Koh or White Magic brands), plus a heavy-duty one (e.g. Nature Direct Tough Guy Cloth)
- glass-cleaning cloth
- general-purpose spray (e.g. Koh Universal Cleaner, TRUEECO Everyday Cleaner, or a 1:1 solution of white vinegar and water)
- glass cleaner (unless your general-purpose cleaner is great for glass)
- magic eraser
- paper towel
- hairspray (for stubborn marks)
- hair dryer.

Floors

A basic kit of floor-cleaning items should include:

- vacuum
- mop, with spare mop pads/heads if applicable – see the Flooring section in the General Cleaning chapter for advice on the best mop for your floors
- floor cleaner – see the Flooring section in the General Cleaning chapter for advice on the best cleaner for your floors
- scraper tool – choose one with a long handle if you can't bend well; these also save time
- microfibre cloth
- grout cleaner (see Cleaning Recipes)
- grout brush.

Note
Alternatively, you can use an all-in-one vacuum/mop.

Walls

A basic kit for getting all those grubby marks and tough stains off walls will include:

- flat microfibre or sponge mop
- cobweb broom
- white vinegar
- glass cleaner
- glass-cleaning cloths
- microfibre cloth
- hairspray
- mop bucket or sink with hot water.

Bathroom/Toilet

Use the basic cleaning kit, plus:

- shaving foam
- Scalex Heavy Duty Home Descaler or citric acid
- rubber gloves
- grout cleaner
- toilet brush
- Bar Keepers Friend Cleanser & Polish Powder (if required).

Kitchen

Use the basic cleaning kit, plus:

- non-scratch scourer or dishwand
- white vinegar
- bicarbonate of soda (bicarb)
- dishwasher tablets
- grout cleaner (for walls)
- aluminium foil.

Shopping List

You may have a lot of these items at home already, so make sure you keep them aside when packing.

- microfibre cloths – you will need at least ten
- glass-cleaning cloths
- non-scratch scourer or dishwand
- general-purpose spray
- glass cleaner (unless your general-purpose spray is also suitable for glass)

- floor cleaner (white vinegar can be used if appropriate for your floor)
- grout cleaner
- Scalex Heavy Duty Home Descaler or citric acid
- Bar Keepers Friend Cleanser & Polish Powder (if required)
- dishwasher tablets
- magic eraser
- bicarbonate of soda (bicarb)
- lemon juice
- white vinegar
- paper towel
- aluminium foil
- hairspray
- shaving foam (if you have tiled floors in the toilet)
- hair dryer
- vacuum (or all-in-one vacuum/mop, e.g. CrossWave)
- floor mop (or all-in-one vacuum/mop, e.g. CrossWave)
- flat microfibre or sponge mop (for walls)
- cobweb broom
- scraper tool
- grout brush
- rubber gloves
- spray bottle
- toilet brush
- mop bucket (if using)
- basket, caddy or bucket to carry your items.

How to start

Figuring out where to begin can be daunting. It is best to start cleaning as you pack, but you may not have time for that. We will give tips on both a pre-planned and last-minute move here so that you can choose which suits your situation. If you can, try to allow 2–3 days for cleaning after you remove all your belongings.

The best place to start is usually the top. Top to bottom is efficient and you won't be making areas dirty again when starting a new task. The floors will be your last job so you don't need to worry about footprints, dust and grime as you clean.

A basic run-down for the order of cleaning is:

1. **ceiling**
2. **cornices/cobwebs**
3. **walls**
4. **surfaces**
5. **floors.**

What to clean

As you remove your belongings from cupboards and cabinets and pack them, carry your basic cleaning kit and use the general-purpose spray and a cloth to wipe out each shelf as it is emptied. This means you won't need to go back later. If you are packing in a rush, you might consider skipping this step and doing it all when your belongings are moved out.

Now is the best time to physically move your belongings to your new home so you can complete your clean efficiently. If you cannot do this, the next best way is to dedicate one room or the garage for your belongings. Choosing a space near the front door or where you're taking it all out will be easiest. Clean the storage room last and move ahead as normal.

1. Ceilings and fans

Exhaust fans should be done at the beginning of your clean as they are likely to throw a lot of dust into the air or onto surrounding surfaces. To clean your exhaust fans, use the deep-clean method in the Family Bathroom/Ensuite chapter.

Ceiling fans will also spread dust. The General Cleaning chapter has specific instructions for cleaning your ceiling fans.

Ensure every light fitting and duct is clean and free from insects and spider webs. You can now spot-clean your ceiling.

Now is also a good time to pop some Scalex or toilet cleaner into your toilet bowls.

2. Walls, windows and doors

Grab your wall kit. Run the cobweb broom over all cornices, wall corners, inside window frames and around doorjambs – dust the tops especially. If you have any brick or rendered walls, use the cobweb broom to brush off any dust. Now run it along the tops of any cabinets. Once you have done inside, do the same outside.

If you have sliding windows, the tracks will likely need some attention. Using the crevice attachment on your vacuum, get out as much debris as you can. This may be enough and you can move to the next step. If there is stuck-on dirt then you may need to delve further – see the General Cleaning chapter for specific instructions.

Clean the interior of your windows, flyscreens and window furnishings. See the General Cleaning chapter for instructions.

Now fill your wall mop bucket or sink with enough hot water to soak the mop pad and about 1 cup of white vinegar. Soak the mop pad and wring out well, attach to the mop and, using large motions, mop the walls. Up and down is best – on the downward stroke, run the mop along the skirting boards too.

Once the mop becomes too dry, soak it and wring again. Repeat as often as necessary, changing the water if it becomes too murky. You can also use this method on the ceiling if required. Otherwise you might like to spot-clean using a cloth and general-purpose spray from the basic kit.

Rachael's *tip*
If the hairspray can't get your marks off, try hand sanitiser or isopropyl alcohol.

Use this same method for the doors in your home.

Once your walls are clean, you may notice tough stains like scuffs on the skirting or rub marks on the walls from furniture. Grab your cloth, squirt some hairspray on it and rub the marks off. Painted surfaces should not be rubbed too vigorously (you don't want to risk removing paint as well) – just enough to remove the mark. You can use this method on your walls, doors, cabinets and skirting boards.

3. Kitchen and surfaces

Take your oven racks out of the oven and start the soaking process. While soaking, use this time to clean your oven, stove, dishwasher and rangehood – see the Kitchen chapter for details on cleaning oven racks and other appliances.

Time for surfaces. Grab your basic cleaning kit. Use the general-purpose spray and a cloth to spray and wipe all your cabinet doors and kickboards, ensuring you are getting the front and all sides. (Use a heavy-duty cloth like the Nature Direct Tough Guy Cloth if your surfaces have a matt finish, or a softer cloth for gloss surfaces.) If you have not already done your cabinet interiors, now is the best time. Change cloths regularly as they become greasy.

Wipe the outside of your appliances, windowsills, taps, benchtops and splashback, inside wardrobes and across the exposed tops of any cabinets and door handles.

Check your oven racks – they are probably ready by now. Use a cloth or scourer to run over each part of the racks. The marks should rub right off. If they don't, let them soak longer and complete this step a little later. Once they are clean, dry them with a towel and pop them back into the oven.

4. Bathroom, sinks and toilets

Grab your bathroom kit now and spray your shower screen and mirror with a glass cleaner. If your screen has a lot of soap scum, you might prefer to use a magic eraser. If you have hard water, you may need to use Bar Keepers Friend Cleanser & Polish Powder or similar. Use your cloth and general-purpose spray to wipe over the shower tracks and frame. (See the Family Bathroom/ Ensuite chapter for specific instructions if you have extra build-up.)

Spray your general-purpose spray over the shower wall tiles and grout. Use a grout brush to scrub away any marks or grime. Use your cloth or shower head to remove the remaining product and mess. Use the same method to clean the shower base, ensuring you clean the drain grate (see the Family Bathroom/Ensuite chapter for more specific advice.) Thoroughly wipe down your bath, vanity top, toilet exterior (including seat) and toilet-roll holder with a bathroom cloth or microfibre cloth.

Grab the bicarb from your kitchen kit and sprinkle a little on each of your sink drains and around the sink surface (laundry, bathroom and kitchen). Now pour or spray white vinegar over it (plug out) for a fizz reaction. Use your scourer or dishwand to clean the sink area and rinse thoroughly with water. Run some hot water to flush the pipes. Dry the sink with a cloth.

Give each toilet a scrub with a toilet brush and flush.

5. Floors

Vacuum your carpets thoroughly, including all edges. If you find you have dents in the carpet from your furniture, you can remove them with a hair dryer or ice cubes. To use a hair dryer, spray a mist of water over the dent then gently blow heated air on the area, using your fingers to manipulate the fibres back to the correct position. To use ice, place a cube on/in each dent and let it melt, then soak up with a white towel and then manipulate the fibres to the correct position with a spoon or your fingers.

Now grab your floor kit. Make sure you only use appropriate methods for the floor you have – for example, floor coverings like laminate cannot get too wet.

If you have tiles, pour grout cleaning solution over all your floor grout. Pouring is a lot easier than spraying (it saves straining your hand). Wait a few minutes, then use your grout brush to scrub each section clean. Clean up the residue with your mop, then mop with clean water as normal.

If you have no tiles or have finished your tiles, mop as per the Flooring section of the General Cleaning chapter. Make sure you put what you need outside first, and mop yourself towards the front door.

Once you have mopped, you have finished the inside of the home!

6. Outdoors

Ensure you have the gardens and outdoor entertaining areas in top shape, mow the lawn, clean any flooring/decking and ensure the garden beds are free of weeds. The Yard chapter has specific advice.

Lastly, clean all your exterior windows. There are hose-on products that may make this easier – Glitz Outdoor Glass Cleaner and 30 Seconds Window Wonder Outdoor Glass Cleaner are products that may help. Otherwise, see the General Cleaning chapter for a guide to cleaning windows and flyscreens.

As you clean, if you find some areas are particularly neglected then refer to the appropriate room chapter for a variety of relevant cleaning hacks.

Vacate/end of lease cleaning checklist

- **WHOLE HOME** – ceilings, light fittings, ceiling fans, ducts, walls, windows (including windowsills), window furnishings, flyscreens, doors, door handles, skirting boards, architraves, floors (including grout)

- **KITCHEN** – exhaust/rangehood, oven, stove, dishwasher, cabinet interiors, cabinet and kickboard exteriors, sink, tapware, splashback, benchtops

- **BEDROOMS** – interior of all wardrobes

- **BATHROOMS** – exhaust fan, tapware, basin/s, inside vanity and any cabinets, shower screen, shower curtain, shower tracks/frame, shower tiles and grout, shower base, drain grates, bath interior

- **TOILETS** – toilet exterior, toilet bowl interior, toilet seat, toilet-roll holder

- **LAUNDRY** – exhaust fan, tub/trough, interior of all cabinets, exterior of all cabinets and kickboards, benchtops

- **LIVING ROOM** – as per whole home

- **DINING ROOM** – as per whole home

- **OUTSIDE** – cobwebs, dust, decking/flooring, concrete, tiles, lawns and weeding

Cleaning *for a* Rental Inspection
• • • • • • • • • • • • • • •

RENTAL INSPECTIONS CAN BE REALLY STRESSFUL even when you know your home is clean. Someone comes into your home and literally rates your ability to look after it – and cleaning is obviously a big part of this.

Your lease will spell out any specific obligations you may have, such as organising professional carpet cleaning and pest control. It's important to read and understand your lease to ensure you know your rights and are meeting your contractual responsibilities. Each state has its own laws, so make sure you're familiar with them. Knowing your rights is essential when you encounter an issue.

The general aim for a rental inspection is to present a clean and tidy home. Keep in mind that you still need to live there, so there is no need to stop doing your normal activities such as washing clothes and cooking food.

Presenting well at an inspection has many benefits for both a tenant and a landlord: a tenant gains a positive rental history, and a landlord/agent can easily identify maintenance issues.

If you've had a bad run and your place is a mess, you might like to start with the My Home is Out of Control chapter. This will get your home up to a normal, lived-in standard. Then you can follow the instructions in the main room chapters of the book to get each room up to scratch.

Areas *to* Focus On
· · · · · · · · · · · · · · · ·

THE HINTS BELOW GIVE YOU some areas to focus on, especially if your time is limited.

Front door/patio

When an agent comes to inspect your home, this is likely to be the first place they see. If they are waiting for you to open the door (or making sure you're not home before they let themselves in), they may take a minute or two to look around. This area will mostly require dusting and cobweb removal – especially around the lights.

Walls

Having clean walls throughout your home really lifts the overall feeling of cleanliness and gives the impression that the home is well looked after.

Skirting boards

Removing dust and scuffs from skirting and architraves is essential. Ensuring this is done not only makes the whole area seem cleaner but also shows your attention to detail.

Yard

You may prefer to outsource this, but a quick mow, weed and sweep-up of mess shows a tenant takes pride in the whole property, not just the interior.

Floors

Clean and tidy floors are essential. Messy floors make even an otherwise spotless home feel uncared for. Floors are also an excellent way for agents to determine lots of maintenance issues. If the floor material is dirty and difficult to see, a problem might be missed. For example, a leaking shower often shows up on the surrounding floor in the bathroom – if the agent can see it, they will be in a better position to arrange to have it fixed quickly.

Window furnishings

Wiping over blinds is another aspect of cleaning that is often forgotten. This is a great way to show your agent you care for your home. For inspection day, open up the windows and window coverings – this ensures lots of light and air makes its way into the home.

Showers

Making sure the glass is clear and the tiles are clean is really important. Showers are one of the more common areas for rental maintenance. If a shower is not cleaned regularly, an agent could easily miss vital maintenance issues like serious mould and leaks.

Windows

Clean windows, tracks and windowsills make identifying areas that need maintenance very easy for an agent. Windows can often have leaks, and being able to identify those leaks easily can prevent serious mould or rot issues. Ensure the sill is wiped to remove dust and any dead insects.

Exhaust fans and/or rangehood

If these go uncleaned they can often break. Tenants sometimes don't realise that their failure to keep up with cleaning could lead to them becoming responsible for any damage.

Sliding door tracks

Keeping sliding door tracks vacuumed can prolong the life of the sliding door. Sliding door rollers can wear, so keeping the track free of debris helps them roll well and means they will require maintenance less often.

If the tracks are full of dirt and debris, the agent may believe any problem with the door is simply an issue of cleanliness, rather than something that requires repair.

Agent's Tips *for* Inspections
· · · · · · · · · · · · · · · ·

EVEN THOUGH HAVING A COMPLETELY SPOTLESS HOME for an inspection is not necessary, it does make an agent's job easier and a tenant more attractive to a landlord. Most agents can tell the difference between a home that is generally well cared for and one that has been cleaned up specifically for the inspection.

Agents often look at exhaust fans. These are regularly forgotten, and the amount of grease and dust in them is a good indicator of how well a tenant is fulfilling their responsibilities.

Dead insects, dirt and dust in windowsills, especially next to the front door, can influence the overall clean feeling of a home.

Inspection cleaning checklist

- **WHOLE HOME** – light fittings, ceiling fans, walls, windows, window furnishings, doors, skirting boards, architraves, floors; remove rubbish and dust; place dirty washing in hampers

- **KITCHEN** – exhaust fan/rangehood, oven, stove, cabinet exteriors, sink, tapware, splashback, benchtops; load the dishwasher or wash the dishes if possible

- **BEDROOMS** – make the bed or pull the covers up; remove clothes and other items from floor

- **BATHROOMS** – exhaust fan, tapware, basin/s, shower glass, shower screen tracks/frame, shower tiles and grout, shower corners (surface mould), drain grate, bath interior

- **TOILETS** – toilet exterior, toilet bowl interior, toilet seat, toilet-roll holder

- **LAUNDRY** – exhaust fan, tub/trough, cabinet exteriors, benchtops

- **LIVING ROOM** – ensure floor is clear

- **DINING ROOM** – ensure floor is clear

- **OUTSIDE** – cobwebs, Dust, flooring/decking, paths, lawns, weeding

While you aren't being judged for the cleanliness of your personal items, it's a good idea to have them put away in appropriate places. This will help your home look and feel tidy, and it will allow the agent to access all areas and make any maintenance decisions.

Preparing *for* an Open Home

OPEN HOMES CAN BE STRESSFUL, whether you are a tenant moving out of a property or an owner-occupier trying to sell your home. Each scenario has its own unique issues to deal with. Here are some tips.

As a tenant

If you are a tenant vacating a property and the owner has scheduled inspections, it is your responsibility to make the home available for inspection by prospective buyers or tenants. (The actual requirements differ in each state. Refer to your state's legislation for details on how much notice an owner must give you before any inspections, and the level of cleanliness expected.) Moving is nerve-racking, and trying to present your home in a positive light while you're packing up can make things even more difficult.

If you have started packing, try to keep all your boxes together, and store them so that prospective tenants or buyers can still see the function of each room.

General cleaning is sufficient for an open-home scenario. It may be wise to remove valuables. Even though most agents take down details of all people who inspect a property, it's better to be safe than sorry. You may also like to remove personal photographs. Removing these items will also limit the amount of dusting to do, making the whole process just that little bit easier.

Make sure you have a front door mat and invest in a carpet square for inside the front door. This will limit your cleaning after the inspection. Bunnings sell carpet squares at a reasonable price.

As an owner

Preparing for an open home when selling your own home will feel a little different. You will want to do everything possible to make your home more appealing. The more appealing it is, the better the offer on it will be – and you may even have a range of offers to choose from.

When people are looking for a home to buy, they are often looking for a way to improve their lifestyle. Exactly what this means will depend on the purchaser, but usually a clean home is a good start. If your home is fresh and clean, people might feel like that is attainable for them too, and that their own lifestyle will therefore be improved.

Is it easy to keep a home spotless when you're preparing to move? Probably not! But these tips will hopefully help cut down the time and energy involved in keeping your home ready for inspections.

- Pack away all of your knick-knacks, including photo frames, to reduce the time you will need to spend dusting. Pack them first so they are out of the way until you are in your own new home.

- Scent can be important, but overpowering scent can be off-putting. Before an open home you can simply boil some cinnamon powder or vanilla essence in water, on the stovetop, for a few minutes. These scents are more often appealing than offensive. They will make your home smell like fresh baked goods without you having to go to the effort of baking.

- The front door and patio are the first areas potential buyers will see. Keep these areas as clean as possible at all times, as people will drive past to pre-inspect the street appeal of your home. Ensure there are no shoes, cobwebs or dead insects hanging around. If you take your shoes off at the door, make sure you have an attractive basket to contain them.

- Neat and tidy gardens provide street appeal immediately. You may like to hire a gardener to take care of this for you to limit the burden. Depending on the season you're selling in, weekly or fortnightly maintenance is best.

- If you have young kids, tidying away toys is a necessity. Make sure all toys are kept in the toy room if you have one. If you don't, consider packing away a large portion of the toys, keeping just a small selection available for the kids to play with. Store them inside tubs in a buffet or in the TV cabinet, for example. If you have no space, use an attractive basket. It's important to choose options that don't make it look like you have no storage space.

- Cook on the barbecue! If you have a barbecue, you can make great use of it by cooking your family meals on it instead of using your stove and oven. Cleaning the stove and oven can be laborious so this tip could save you hours over your sale period. Keeping your meals fairly basic will also help keep the kitchen in top order without the need to be constantly cleaning.

- The more you can pack and store offsite, or in the garage, the more appealing your home will be to most people, especially if you're advertising your home as 'move-in ready'. You might have friends or family who can give up some space for a short time, or you could hire a storage unit. There are businesses that will bring a moving container to your home; once you have packed it, they will take it away and store it offsite. Storing packed items offsite will make your home a lot easier to clean, as there won't be as much work in tidying up or working around items.

cleaning schedule

take back control with a

personalised cleaning schedule

How to **Create a Schedule**

· · · · · · · · · · · · · · · · ·

DESIGNING A CLEANING SCHEDULE is a lot easier than you might think. A schedule works best when it is designed around your own life – you will be more likely to stick to it and it will require less effort.

Start by listing every cleaning task you want to get done daily. Then list the tasks that you need to do once a week. Don't overcomplicate the list. If you want to clean one room a day, then just list that room. You probably know what cleaning this room involves, so you don't need to write each step down.

List the tasks that you are happy to do fortnightly or monthly – cleaning the oven, cleaning skirting boards or changing bed linen, for example. (These will differ depending on your needs.)

Grab a blank calendar, or write out the days of the week across the top of a sheet of paper, then add four rows underneath to represent four weeks of cleaning. (See the blank schedule below for layout advice.) Working on a four-weekly rotating schedule is a really easy way to create your cleaning schedule, rather than working to calendar months that have differing starting days and different numbers of days.

Mark each of your busy days with a star. This will act as a visual reminder to not add too many tasks to those days. A busy day might be when you have after-school activities with the kids or similar.

Now refer to your task list and add in each daily task. Start with the weekly tasks and repeat them over the following three weeks.

Next, add in your fortnightly tasks. Add any monthly tasks once, anywhere within the four-weekly schedule – this is close enough to monthly.

For tasks you want to do less frequently than monthly, add an entry for 'Intermittent task', and pick one from your list each time that comes around. List your intermittent tasks at the side or bottom of the schedule sheet.

You should now have a user-friendly schedule to work from to keep your home clean and tidy, with less daily effort and no catch-ups on the weekends.

It's a good idea to laminate your list, or cover it with plastic, so you can use a whiteboard marker to mark off the completed tasks. This way everyone in the family can see which jobs are outstanding and can complete them.

If more than one person is expected to complete these tasks, you might like to colour-code them so each person can easily recognise their daily task. Cross off the days as you go. At the end of the four weeks, just wipe the marker off and start again.

Cleaning Schedule Example

MONDAY	TUESDAY	WEDNESDAY	THURSDAY	FRIDAY	SATURDAY	SUNDAY
Washing Tidy Dining/Entry Dust Cornices & Skirting Boards Intermittent Tasks	Washing Tidy Vaccum Mop Bedrooms Toy Room Alcove	Washing Tidy Kitchen Oven Living/Lounge	Washing Tidy Bathroom Ensuite Laundry Study	Washing Tidy Vaccum Mop	Washing Tidy	Washing Tidy
Washing Tidy Dining/Entry Dust Wash Walls	Washing Tidy Vaccum Mop Bedrooms Toy Room Alcove	Washing Tidy Kitchen Living/Lounge	Washing Tidy Bathroom Ensuite Laundry Study	Washing Tidy Vaccum Mop	Washing Tidy	Washing Tidy
Washing Tidy Dining/Entry Dust Cornices & Skirting Boards	Washing Tidy Vaccum Mop Bedrooms Toy Room Alcove	Washing Tidy Kitchen Living/Lounge	Washing Tidy Bathroom Ensuite Laundry Study	Washing Tidy Vaccum Mop	Washing Tidy	Washing Tidy
Washing Tidy Dining/Entry Dust Wash Walls	Washing Tidy Vaccum Mop Bedrooms Toy Room Alcove	Washing Tidy Living/Lounge	Washing Tidy Bathroom Ensuite Laundry Study	Washing Tidy Vaccum Mop	Washing Tidy	Washing Tidy

Cleaning Schedule Template

MONDAY	TUESDAY	WEDNESDAY	THURSDAY	FRIDAY	SATURDAY	SUNDAY

cleaning
recipes

cheap, easy and effective

solutions for your home

General-purpose Bathroom Spray

. . . .

500 ml warm water

2 tablespoons bicarbonate of soda

1/4 cup white vinegar

Few drops essential oil (optional)

Slowly add the bicarb and vinegar to the water, adding essential oils for scent if desired. Pour into a spray bottle and it's good to go.

Glass and Stainless Steel Cleaner

. . . .

100 ml white vinegar

300 ml water

Combine 1 part vinegar to 3 parts water. Keep in a spray bottle. Spray onto glass or stainless steel and wipe with a soft microfibre cloth.

Grout Cleaner

. . . .

1/4 cup bicarbonate of soda

1/3 cup lemon juice

1/4 cup white vinegar

7 cups water

Combine all ingredients. You can scale this recipe up or down as required, but try not to change the ratios as the bicarb can leave a residue. Use a spray bottle or a screw-top bottle to store.

Polident Solution

· · · · · · · · · · · · · · ·

1 Polident 3 Minute Daily Cleanser tablet

1 cup warm water

Place tablet and warm water inside a spray bottle. Let the tablet dissolve, then place the trigger nozzle on the bottle. Use immediately. If not using straightaway, remove the trigger – pressure may build in the bottle if the trigger remains in place, causing leaks.

Toilet Bombs

· · · · · · · · · · · · · · ·

2 cups bicarbonate of soda

2/3 cup citric acid

15 drops essential oils

Water

Mix together the bicarb, citric acid and essential oils. Gradually add very small amounts of water until the mixture sticks together, but don't let it get gluggy. Spoon the mixture into an ice-cube tray (one just for cleaning products) and use the back of the spoon to pack it in firmly. Leave overnight to dry. Pop into a container and use as needed.

Washing Powder

· · · · · · · · · · · · · · · · ·

100 g soap flakes (e.g. Lux brand) or grated soap

200 g bicarbonate of soda

200 g washing soda (sodium carbonate, e.g. Lectric brand)

Few drops essential oils (optional)

Mix together ingredients, including essential oils for scent if desired.
Use 1–2 tablespoons per load. Store in a container of your choosing.

odour-eliminating
recipes

quick and easy hacks to
send that pong packing

Carpet Deodoriser

・・・・・・・・・・・・・・・

1 cup bicarbonate of soda

10–15 drops essential oils

Combine bicarb and essential oils. Place the mixture into a shaker with large holes. (Note that this container will no longer be suitable for food.) Shake the powder onto your carpet at night and vacuum up in the morning.

Pet Odour Eliminator

・・・・・・・・・・・・・・・

350 ml water

100 ml white vinegar

7 drops of lemon oil, or other essential oil as preferred

Combine ingredients in a spray bottle. Mist your room, and spray fabrics from a distance so the mist spreads and removes the odour.

Room Spray

・・・・・・・・・・・・・・・

Water

10–15 drops essential oils

In a spray bottle, combine water and essential oils. Do not overfill the bottle – you will need sufficient space to mix the ingredients. Shake the bottle well before spraying the rooms of your home.

Scent Pack

· · · · · · · · · · · · · · · · ·

Fill a small organza bag with dried lavender petals, dried potpourri or similar. Close the bag and tie it tightly. If you have some fabric scraps, you can machine- or hand-sew the bags yourself instead of using organza bags. Ensure you use a fabric that breathes well.

Stovetop Potpourri

· · · · · · · · · · · · · · · · · ·

Water

1 orange, sliced

3–4 whole cloves, or a pinch of ground cloves

1 cinnamon stick, or ¼ teaspoon ground cinnamon

1 slice fresh ginger, or ½ teaspoon ground ginger

In a small saucepan, combine water, orange slices, cloves, cinnamon and ginger. Bring the mixture to the boil, then return to low heat to allow the scent to permeate the home. Add water as required – don't let it boil dry.

index

notes

add your own cleaning tips here,
and don't forget to share them with
the Mums Who community online

Tip:

_____

_____

_____

_____

_____

Tip:

_____

_____

_____

_____

_____

Tip:

_____

_____

_____

_____

_____

Tip:

Tip:

Tip:

Tip:

Tip:

Tip:

Tip:

Tip:

Tip:

Tip:

Tip:

Tip:

Acknowledgements

· · · · · · · · · · · · · · · · ·

WE WOULD LIKE TO THANK the members of all our Mums Who groups for helping us to create such a positive and supportive community.

Our admin team – Elise, Gill and Emma – along with our team moderators (current and past): you ladies are amazing! Your dedication to helping us keep the groups running smoothly is phenomenal and never taken for granted.

We would like to thank each of our families for their support while we have built the Mums Who brand. Many, many hours have gone into creating the groups, Facebook page, Instagram page, website and now this book. We appreciate your love and patience while we have constantly had our faces in our phones.